# Surya Dev

## The Sun God

How to Energize SUN in your life
with Vedic Astrology

Surya Chalisa, Surya Arti, Surya Mantra,
Surya Vrat Katha, and Remedies for a
Malefic Sun in your Horoscope/Birth Chart



**Acharya Tewari**

The Chalisa, Mantras, and other prayers in Hindi and Sanskrit have been passed on from word of mouth to a written from since times immemorial. Though, no substantial proof of authorship is known thus far, these have been a part of Hindu rituals and prayers till date. Our sincere effort is to provide transliteration and to interpret them into simple comprehensible English so that a wider audience may benefits from Vedic astrology. For a professional assessment of your horoscope/birth chart and further guidance, always seek consultation from an experienced and expert Vedic astrologer.

Interior and Cover designed by
Richa Bargotra

First edition: 2023

# Dedicated To

It is nearly impossible to express my gratitude to my ancestors, parents, wife, and daughter for guiding me to be a vessel that may provide solace or a feasible solution to someone's problems. They have provided me with unending, genuine, and consistent support as I compiled this information for you. Though I am grateful to many more people, time and space constraints force me to stop here.

Peace!

We strongly advise consulting an experienced and expert Vedic astrologer for professional assessment of your horoscope and further guidance. Please watch YouTube videos for correct pronuciation of the Chalisa, mantras, chants etc.

ॐ असतो मा सद्गमय।
तमसो मा ज्योतिर्गमय।
मृत्योर्मा अमृतं गमय।
ॐ शान्तिः शान्तिः शान्तिः।।

*asato ma sadgamaya*
*tamaso ma jyotirgamaya*
*mrtyorma amrtam gamaya*
*om shanti shanti shanti.*

Lead me from the unreal to the ultimate truth.
Lead me from darkness to light.
Lead me from death to immortality

We strongly advise consulting an experienced and expert Vedic astrologer for professional assessment of your horoscope and further guidance. Please watch YouTube videos for correct pronuciation of the Chalisa, mantras, chants etc.

# Table of Contents



We strongly advise consulting an experienced and expert Vedic astrologer for professional assessment of your horoscope and further guidance. Please watch YouTube videos for correct pronuciation of the Chalisa, mantras, chants etc.

# Preface

Sun was one of the first divine objects that human race worshiped. In fact, sun worship is thought to be one of the world's oldest religions, dating back to prehistoric times. Several religions and ethnic groups not only regard the Sun as significant but also worship deities who represent the Sun or one of its characteristics, such as strength, warmth, and power.

In *Vedic* astrology the sun is known as *Surya* or *Ravi*. The sacred holy texts "*Puranas*" describe the *Surya* (Sun) as one who illuminates the universe with its light. As per *Purāṇic* literature, *Surya* is the son of *Kaśyapaprajāpati* and *Aditi*. Sun God is also referred to as *Bhaskar, Ark, Arun, Bhanu, Dinakar, Ravi, Dhinakar or Dhinakrit, Thanpna,* and *Pusha* by Hindus. The first mention of sun worship can be found in the *Rig-Vedas*, our monumental ancient collections of hymns, where sun worship is couched in poetic and metaphoric expressions.

Surya is the preserver and soul of all things stationary and moving and is thus known as the creator of everything;

enlivened by him, men perform their work; he is far-seeing, all-seeing, and beholds all living things, as well as the good and evil moral deeds. Sage *Patanjali*, who promoted yogic philosophy, placed a high value on the *Sūryanamaskār* (the ten-step yogic postures done in obeyance of the Sun God). *Sūryanamaskār* strengthens one's bones, cures illness, no matter how severe, cleanses the devotee of his sins, and bestows progeny, wealth, good health, and long life. *Surya* is the most brilliant leading light, the glowing ball of light that is sent to humanity. He is portrayed as the gods' eye, which observes all worldly actions. He sustains and energizes the entire creation with his light. The Sun is imaged poetically as the God riding in his chariot drawn by seven white horses, while *Aruna* serves as the charioteer. It was thought that the sun and moon revolved around Mount *Mahmeru*.

The text in Vedic astrology have also called sun as *Atmakaraka*. This is a Sanskrit word, where "*atma*" means souls and "*karaka*" pertains to indicator. Thus, sun is the indicator of the soul and giver of life. The Sun is supposed to represent father, ego, honors, status, fame, heart, eyes, general vitality, respect, and power. *Surya Dev* provides us with vitality, resistance, and immunity, and it oversees our physical makeup - our body's constitution. Vedic astrology also believes that Sun strongly influences the human spine. *Pingala Nadi*, which represents the Sun in our spine, begins at the base of the spine (on the right side), and ends in the right nostril. The Sun is associated with men's right and women's left eyes. The Sun rules the heart, liver, lungs, head (brain), nerves, and bones. A malefic Sun causes unstable blood pressure, gastrointestinal issues, predisposes to dia-

We strongly advise consulting an experienced and expert Vedic astrologer for professional assessment of your horoscope and further guidance. Please watch YouTube videos for correct pronuciation of the Chalisa, mantras, chants etc.

betes, cardiac thrombosis, frequent facial eruptions, mental problems caused by overthinking, epilepsy, and disorders caused by aggravated bile.

*Surya Dev* is considered a living God to whom all can see, perceive, and pray. The Vedas revere him as a witness (*Sakshi*) to all events. He spends one month in each zodiac sign and completes a round of all 12 zodiac signs in 365 days. The Sun is in its strongest placement directly overhead in the 10th House. The Sun also does well in the growing houses, which are the 3rd, 6th, and 11th. Moon, Mars, and Jupiter are Sun's natural allies, while Venus, Saturn, *Rahu*, and *Ketu* are its natural enemies. Sun is particularly beneficial for the fire signs, Aries, Leo, and Sagittarius. The gemstone that is considered auspicious for *Surya Dev* is the red ruby stone.

# CHAPTER 1

# Introduction

|| श्री गणेशाय नमः ||

This succinct book is dedicated to *Surya Dev* or the Sun God, who is the source of life for everything in our universe. Hindus revere the Sun God, as a significant divinity who removes the darkness of ignorance and bestows wisdom, much as how the morning dispels the darkness of the realms. The Sun is said to be the source of **all** knowledge. As per the ancient *Vedic* scriptures Sun is also named as *Sarvati Sakshi Bhutam* which means the ever-watching witness to everything happening on mother earth. As the sun shines constantly on the earth, nothing can be hidden from him. *Surya Dev* is portrayed as a red male with three eyes and four arms who rides in a chariot drawn by seven mares. Two of *Surya's* hands are holding water lilies, and he inspires his worshippers with his third hand while blessing them with his fourth.

We strongly advise consulting an experienced and expert Vedic astrologer for professional assessment of your horoscope and further guidance. Please watch YouTube videos for correct pronuciation of the Chalisa, mantras, chants etc.

According to *Vedic* Astrology, the Sun governs your relationship with your father, your father's health, and any benefits you may receive from your father. Aside from the foregoing, the Sun governs your interactions with the government, government agencies, and government corporations. The Sun God bestows administrative and leadership abilities. The Sun represents administrators and judges.

In India, *Surya Dev* is revered as a benevolent deity who can heal the sick. People still place the Sun symbol over the home's main entrance or shops because they believe it will bring them good fortune. According to Hindu folklore, Lord *Ram* worshiped *Surya* Dev. Even *Karna* (a famous warrior in the epic *Mahabharata*) was a devout worshipper of *Surya Dev* (Sun God). There are numerous temples devoted to *Surya Dev's* worship where he is worshiped early in the morning, particularly during Hindu festivals such as *Makar Sankranti, Ratha Saptami, Chhath*, and *Samba Dashami*. The Sun God is also known as "*Mitra* "because of his nourishing qualities. *Surya Dev*, in his *Mitra* form, is primarily worshiped in Gujarat, India. In India, there are several festivals dedicated to the Sun God. The following are the most important:

- ***Makara Sankranti/Pongal***: This is considered as one of the largest and most popular festivals honoring the Sun God. People pray to and thank the Sun God for a bountiful harvest. The first grains are dedicated to him.
- ***Chhath***: Another famous festival honoring the Sun God. It is primarily observed in Bihar and Jharkhand but also in parts of Uttar Pradesh and Nepal.

- ***Surya Jayanti/Ratha Saptami***: This festival honors the Sun God's power. It is commemorated on the seventh day of Magha, the bright half of the Hindu month.
- ***Samba Dashami***: This festival commemorates *Samba* (Lord *Krishna's* son), who was cured of leprosy after praying to *Surya Dev*.

## GENERAL ATTRIBUTES OF SURYA DEV (SUN GOD) AS PER VEDIC ASTROLOGY

**Color:** Vermillion Red

**Day: Sunday**

**God / Deity:** Lord *Shiva* and Goddess *Parvati*

**Gemstone:** Ruby-*Manik*

**Finger:** Ring, Middle

**Metal:** Gold or Copper

**Direction:** East

**Rashis:** Leo-*Simha*

**Ucch (Exalted) Rashi:** Aries-*Mesh*

**Neech (Falling) Rashi:** Libra-*Tula*

**Mantra:** *Om Bhaskaraya Namah*

**Yantra:** *Surya Yantra*

**Rudraksha**: 12 *Mukhi*

We strongly advise consulting an experienced and expert Vedic astrologer for professional assessment of your horoscope and further guidance. Please watch YouTube videos for correct pronuciation of the Chalisa, mantras, chants etc.

# CHAPTER 2

# Surya Chalisa

*Surya Dev Chalisa* (*Chalisa* means 40 Lines in Ode to a deity) is a devotional hymn dedicated to the God of Sun, the supreme soul who provides light and warmth to the world. The ancient *Vedic* scriptures like *Vedas* and *Puranas* have emphasized the significance of worshiping *Surya Dev*. *Surya Puja* promotes mental and physical well-being. Devotees recite it to achieve peace, joy, and success in their life. *Surya Chalisa* produces a lot of energy in your body when chanted aloud. On festivals honoring *Shri Surya Dev*, many recite the *Surya Dev Chalisa*.

We strongly advise consulting an experienced and expert Vedic astrologer for professional assessment of your horoscope and further guidance. Please watch YouTube videos for correct pronuciation of the Chalisa, mantras, chants etc.

## Surya Dev Chalisa I

### || दोहा || Preliminary prayer

कनक बदन कुण्डल मकर, मुक्ता माला अङ्ग,
पद्मासन स्थित ध्याइए, शंख चक्र के सङ्ग।।

***kanaka badana kundala makara, mukta mala anga,***
***padmasana sthita dhyaie, shankha chakra ke sanga*** ||

**Meaning:** *Shri Surya Dev!* Thou body is made of gold; your ears adorn ornaments of Capricorn, your neck embellishes beaded adornments; Your hands are adorned with the sacred wheels of *chakra* and *shanka*, and you are seated on a lotus.

|| चौपाई 1 ||

जय सविता जय जयति दिवाकर!।
सहस्त्रांशु! सप्ताश्व तिमिरहर।।
भानु! पतंग! मरीची! भास्कर!।
सविता हंस! सुनूर विभाकर ।।

***jaya savita jaya jayati divakara!*** |
***sahastranshu! saptashva timirahara*** ||
***bhanu! patanga! marichi! bhaskara!*** |
***savita hansa! sunura vibhakara*** ||

**Meaning:** *Shri Surya Dev!* Victory to you! Thou are the blessed one! Triumph to you, the God of light! Thou have thousand rays! You ride on seven celestial horses! Thou

We strongly advise consulting an experienced and expert Vedic astrologer for professional assessment of your horoscope and further guidance. Please watch YouTube videos for correct pronuciation of the Chalisa, mantras, chants etc.

eliminate darkness! You are the king! You are God! You are the ray of light! You are illumination! Like a swan sorting out milk, you take out the golden sparkle and shower on us.

|| चौपाई 2 ||

विवस्वान! आदित्य! विकर्तन ।
मार्तण्ड हरिरूप विरोचन ।।
अम्बरमणि! खग! रवि कहलाते ।
वेद हिरण्यगर्भ कह गाते ।।

***vivasvana! aditya! vikartana*** |
***martanda harirupa virochana*** ||
***ambaramani! khaga! ravi kahalate*** |
***veda hiranyagarbha kaha gate*** ||

**Meaning:** *Shri Surya Dev!* You are the Sun God! Thou are the primary one! You disperse rays! You appeared from the void! You appear like *Shri Narayana*! Thou are the glowing one! You are a celestial jewel! Thou are the sun! *Ravi* (who roars) is thy name! You are admired as the golden one who is a visible source of our universe!

|| चौपाई 3 ||

सहस्त्रांशु प्रद्द्योतन, कहिकहि ।
मुनिगन होत प्रसन्न मोदलहि ।।
अरुण सदृश सारथी मनोहर ।
हांकत हय साता चढ़ि रथ पर ।।

We strongly advise consulting an experienced and expert Vedic astrologer for professional assessment of your horoscope and further guidance. Please watch YouTube videos for correct pronuciation of the Chalisa, mantras, chants etc.

***sahastranshu pradyotana, kahikahi |***
***munigana hota prasanna modalahi ||***
***aruna sadrisha sarathi manohara |***
***hankata haya sata chati ratha para ||***

**Meaning:** *Shri Surya Dev!* You have a thousand brilliant rays! You appear bright crimson in the sky! The sages and their groups are delighted to see you. Your rise in the sky as a crimson ball is very pleasing. Thou are very vigilant, and your chariot climbs the sky with seven horses.

|| चौपाई 4 ||

मंडल की महिमा अति न्यारी ।
तेज रूप केरी बलिहारी ।।
उच्चौः श्रवा सदृश हय जोते ।
देखि पुरन्दर लज्जित होते ।।

***mandala ki mahima ati nyari |***
***teja rupa keri balihari ||***
***uchchaih-shrava sadrisha haya jote |***
***dekhi purandara lajjita hote ||***

**Meaning:** *Shri Surya Dev!* The glory possessed by your group, the *Surya Mandal* or galaxy, is revered by all. We all are consumed by your gleaming and glittering form. The horse named *Shrava* adorns the highest position in your Chariot. [*Shrava* is a believed to be a white horse with wings, and it belonged to Lord Indra]. *Shrava* runs so fast that it even humbles Indra on seeing your radiance

We strongly advise consulting an experienced and expert Vedic astrologer for professional assessment of your horoscope and further guidance. Please watch YouTube videos for correct pronuciation of the Chalisa, mantras, chants etc.

|| चौपाई 5 ||

मित्र मरीचि भानु अरुण भास्कर ।
सविता सूर्य अर्क खग कलिकर ।।
पूषा रवि आदित्य नाम लै ।
हिरण्यगर्भाय नमः कहिकै ।।

***mitra marichi bhanu aruna bhaskara |***
***savita surya arka khaga kalikara ||***
***pusha ravi aditya nama lai |***
***hiranyagarbhaya namah kahikai ||***

**Meaning:** *Shri Surya Dev!* Thou are our friend and a ray of light! You are the brilliance! You are crimson! You glitter and create light! Thou are the blessed one! *Surya*, the sun! Thou move in the sky! You eliminate darkness! Your other names are *Pusha, Ravi* and *Aditya*. We salute you and honor your golden physical form.

|| चौपाई 6 ||

द्वादस नाम प्रेम सों गावैं ।
मस्तक बारह बार नवावैं ।।
चार पदारथ जन सो पावै ।
दुःख दारिद्र अघ पुंज नसावै ।।

***dvadasa nama prema som gavaim |***
***mastaka baraha bara navavaim ||***
***chara padaratha jana so pavai |***
***duhkha daridra agha punja nasavai ||***

**Meaning:** *Shri Surya Dev!* Lord *Indra* affectionately venerates you with twelve names; Thou rule all twelve months. You bestow us with four virtues (strength, energy, hard labor, and *moksha*) and your rays rightfully obliterate sorrow and deprivation.

|| चौपाई 7 ||

नमस्कार को चमत्कार यह ।
विधि हरिहर को कृपासार यह ।।
सेवै भानु तुमहिं मन लाई ।
अष्टसिद्धि नवनिधि तेहिं पाई ।।

***namaskara ko chamatkara yaha |***
***vidhi harihara ko kripasara yaha ||***
***sevai bhanu tumahim mana lai |***
***ashtasiddhi navanidhi tehim pai ||***

**Meaning:** *Shri Surya Dev!* Accept grateful salutations for making miracles happen in our life! As the amalgamation of *Hari* and *Hara* (i.e. (*Vishnu* and *Shiva*), you alleviate the terrible effects of destiny. You provide service through your rays and brightness! Thou bestow on us eight yogic *siddhis* and *Nava Nidhis* (nine sources of wealth)

- The right yogic attributes are ***Aṇimā*** (ability to reduce body size to that of an atom), ***Mahima*** (ability to increase body size to infinity), ***Garima*** (ability to make the body infinitely heavy), ***Laghima*** (ability to make the body substantially light), ***Prāpti*** (ability to be anywhere,

We strongly advise consulting an experienced and expert Vedic astrologer for professional assessment of your horoscope and further guidance. Please watch YouTube videos for correct pronuciation of the Chalisa, mantras, chants etc.

at will or ability to obtain anything desired), ***Prākāmya*** (realizing one's desires), ***Iṣiṭva*** (supremacy over nature) and ***Vaśitva*** (possessing control over natural forces)

- *The Nava nidhis* (Nine types of wealth) are symbolized as ***Maha-Padma*** (great lotus flower), ***Padma*** (a lake in Himalayas or a regular lotus), ***Shankha*** (conch shell), ***Makara*** (Antimony or crocodile), ***Kachchapa*** (turtle shell or a tortoise), ***Kumud*** (precious stone), ***Kunda*** (Arsenic/Jasmine), ***Nila*** (sapphire) and ***Kharva*** (cups/ utensils baked in fire).

|| चौपाई 8 ||

बारह नाम उच्चारन करते ।
सहस जनम के पातक टरते ।।
उपाख्यान जो करते तवजन ।
रिपु सों जमलहते सोतेहि छन ।।

***baraha nama uchcharana karate |***
***sahasa janama ke pataka tarate ||***
***upakhyana jo karate tavajana |***
***ripu som jamalahate sotehi chhana ||***

**Meaning:** *Shri Surya Dev!* People who chant your twelve names will be relieved of all their misfortunes resulting from their misdeeds in life. Thunder and rain fall on ground when your names are chanted! You are the enemy of frozen water bodies, causing them to melt.

- The twelve names of *Surya Dev* to be recited are ***Om Mithraya Namaha*** (friend), ***Om Ravaye Namaha*** (one who roars), ***Om Suryaya Namaha*** (brilliant), ***Om Bhanave Namaha*** (bright), ***Om Khagaya Namaha*** (one who moves in the sky), ***Om Pushne Namaha*** (nourisher of all), ***Om Hiranya Garbhaya Namaha*** (the golden source), ***Om Marichaye Namaha*** (dawn), ***Om Adityaya Namaha*** (son of *Aditi*), ***Om Savitre Namaha*** (the riser), ***Om Arkaya Namaha*** (praiseworthy) and ***Om Bhaskaraya Namaha*** (one who is enlightening)

|| चौपाई 9 ||

धन सुत जुत परिवार बढ़तु है ।
प्रबल मोह को फंद कटतु है ।।
अर्क शीश को रक्षा करते ।
रवि ललाट पर नित्य बिहरते ।।

***dhana suta juta parivara badhatu hai*** |
***prabala moha ko phanda katatu hai*** ||
***arka shisha ko raksha karate*** |
***ravi lalata para nitya biharate*** ||

**Meaning:** *Shri Surya Dev!* We, our children, and our family prosper when we recite your names! The more we become secure in your power, the freer we feel from our obligations. You guard *Shish*, an extract of light that glistens like glass and emits light daily from your head.

We strongly advise consulting an experienced and expert Vedic astrologer for professional assessment of your horoscope and further guidance. Please watch YouTube videos for correct pronuciation of the Chalisa, mantras, chants etc.

|| चौपाई 10 ||

सूर्य नेत्र पर नित्य विराजत ।
कर्ण देस पर दिनकर छाजत ।।
भानु नासिका वासकरहुनित ।
भास्कर करत सदा मुखको हित ।।

***surya netra para nitya virajata |***
***karna desa para dinakara chhajata ||***
***bhanu nasika vasakarahunita |***
***bhaskara karata sada mukhako hita ||***

**Meaning:** *Shri Surya Dev!* You reign in our eyes! You are in ears! You prevail in our nostrils as pleasant aroma! You are the pleasant smell in our nostrils! Good things come to those who gaze at your glorious face (form).

|| चौपाई 11 ||

ओंठ रहैं पर्जन्य हमारे ।
रसना बीच तीक्ष्ण बस प्यारे ।।
कंठ सुवर्ण रेत की शोभा ।
तिग्म तेजसः कांधे लोभा ।।

***ontha rahaim parjanya hamare |***
***rasana bicha tikshna basa pyare ||***
***kantha suvarna reta ki shobha |***
***tigma tejasah kandhe lobha ||***

**Meaning:** *Shri Surya Dev!* You make rain and pour it down on us! All living beings flourish and rejoice in rains! Your throat is beautiful and graceful, and it appears to be a powerful weapon on your shoulders!

|| चौपाई 12 ||

पूषां बाहू मित्र पीठहिं पर ।
त्वष्टा वरुण रहत सुउष्णकर ।।
युगल हाथ पर रक्षा कारन ।
भानुमान उरसर्म सुउदरचन ।।

***pusham bahu mitra pithahim para |***
***tvashta varuna rahata suushnakara ||***
***yugala hatha para raksha karana |***
***bhanumana urasarma suudarachana ||***

**Meaning:** *Shri Surya Dev!* Like a friend, your valiant arms provide warmth! The invisible *Varuna* (rain God) also dwells in you! Your hands are only there to protect us! Your entire body is made of bright light!

|| चौपाई 13 ||

बसत नाभि आदित्य मनोहर ।
कटिमंह, रहत मन मुदभर ।।
जंघा गोपति सविता बासा ।
गुप्त दिवाकर करत हुलासा ।।

We strongly advise consulting an experienced and expert Vedic astrologer for professional assessment of your horoscope and further guidance. Please watch YouTube videos for correct pronuciation of the Chalisa, mantras, chants etc.

***basata nabhi aditya manohara |***
***katimanha, rahata mana mudabhara ||***
***jangha gopati savita basa |***
***gupta divakara karata hulasa ||***

**Meaning:** *Shri Surya Dev!* Your abdomen is the source of the rays that captivate our minds! It serves as our minds' focus. *Shri Maha-Vishnu* rules over your thighs! Your dazzling rays dispel all darkness!

|| चौपाई 14 ||

विवस्वान पद की रखवारी ।
बाहर बसते नित तम हारी ।।
सहस्त्रांशु सर्वांग सम्हारै ।
रक्षा कवच विचित्र विचारे ।।

***vivasvana pada ki rakhavari |***
***bahara basate nita tama hari ||***
***sahastranshu sarvanga sanharai |***
***raksha kavacha vichitra vichare ||***

**Meaning:** *Shri Surya Dev!* We bow down at your feet to worship! You win the battle against the darkness! Your thousands of rays dispel all forms of darkness! It is difficult for anyone to see through your defensive armor.

We strongly advise consulting an experienced and expert Vedic astrologer for professional assessment of your horoscope and further guidance. Please watch YouTube videos for correct pronuciation of the Chalisa, mantras, chants etc.

## || चौपाई 15 ||

अस जोजन अपने मन माहीं ।
भय जगबीच करहुं तेहि नाहीं ।।
दद्रु कुष्ठ तेहिं कबहु न व्यापै ।
जोजन याको मन मंह जापै ।।

***asa jojana apane mana mahim |***
***bhaya jagabicha karahum tehi nahim ||***
***dadru kushtha tehim kabahu na vyapai |***
***jojana yako mana manha japai ||***

**Meaning:** *Shri Surya Dev!* Anyone who constantly thinks of and prays to the Sun God should not be afraid of anything in this world. Anyone who chants the Sun God's attributes will be free of skin disease and leprosy. The one who spreads golden rays, we salute you!

## || चौपाई 16 ||

अंधकार जग का जो हरता ।
नव प्रकाश से आनन्द भरता ।।
ग्रह गन ग्रसि न मिटावत जाही ।
कोटि बार मैं प्रनवौं ताही ।।

***andhakara jaga ka jo harata |***
***nava prakasha se ananda bharata ||***
***graha gana grasi na mitavata jahi |***
***koti bara maim pranavaum tahi ||***

We strongly advise consulting an experienced and expert Vedic astrologer for professional assessment of your horoscope and further guidance. Please watch YouTube videos for correct pronuciation of the Chalisa, mantras, chants etc.

**Meaning:** *Shri Surya Dev!* You expel all the darkness from the world! You radiate light with joy and are incredibly bright! In comparison to you, the brightness of the other planets appears dim! You belong to a different category than the other planets!

|| चौपाई 17 ||

मंद सदृश सुत जग में जाके ।
धर्मराज सम अद्भुत बांके ।।
धन्य–धन्य तुम दिनमनि देवा ।
किया करत सुरमुनि नर सेवा ।।

***manda sadrisha suta jaga mem jake|***
***dharmaraja sama adbhuta banke ||***
***dhanya-dhanya tuma dinamani deva |***
***kiya karata suramuni nara seva ||***

**Meaning:** Despite being like sunlight, *Shri Shani Dev* appeared dull; He ascended to the rank of *Yama*, the Lord of *Dharma*; *Shri Shani Dev* is as magnificent as *Shri Surya Dev* because of his penance to Lord *Shiva*! We are grateful to you, *Shri Surya Dev,* the God of days! Everyone, including *devas*, sages, and humans, is always at your disposal.

|| चौपाई 18 ||

भक्ति भावयुत पूर्ण नियम सों ।
दूर हटतसो भवके भ्रम सों ।।
परम धन्य सों नर तनधारी ।
हैं प्रसन्न जेहि पर तम हारी ।।

We strongly advise consulting an experienced and expert Vedic astrologer for professional assessment of your horoscope and further guidance. Please watch YouTube videos for correct pronuciation of the Chalisa, mantras, chants etc.

***bhakti bhavayuta purna niyama som |***
***dura hatataso bhavake bhrama som ||***
***parama dhanya som nara tanadhari |***
***haim prasanna jehi para tama hari ||***

**Meaning:** *Shri Surya Dev!* People who worship you fervently are blessed with salvation, and all their illusions are dispelled. You are pleased with their devotion, and you shower your blessings on them, bringing the light of happiness into their lives by removing the darkness of their worries and sorrows.

|| चौपाई 19 ||

अरुण माघ महं सूर्य फाल्गुन ।
मधु वेदांग नाम रवि उदयन ।।
भानु उदय बैसाख गिनावै ।
ज्येष्ठ इन्द्र आषाढ़ रवि गावै ।।

***aruna magha maham surya phalguna |***
***madhu vedanga nama ravi udayana ||***
***bhanu udaya baisakha ginavai |***
***jyeshtha indra ashadha ravi gavai ||***

**Meaning:** *Shri Surya Dev!* You are ***Arun***, the crimson sun, in the month of ***Magha***. You are ***Surya***, in the month of ***Phalguni***. You are ***Vedanga*** in the month of ***Madhu***, the one who is a part of the *Vedas (*the holy scriptures). You are known as ***Ravi*** when it is time to rise. You are known as ***Bhanu***, the brightness, at the

We strongly advise consulting an experienced and expert Vedic astrologer for professional assessment of your horoscope and further guidance. Please watch YouTube videos for correct pronuciation of the Chalisa, mantras, chants etc.

start of ***Baisaka***: You are ***Indra*** during the ***Jyeshta*** month: You are ***Ravi*** during the month of ***Ashada***.

- Please see Appendix for how *Surya Dev* is worshipped according to the ancient Hindu calendar.

|| चौपाई 20 ||

यम भादों आश्विन हिमरेता ।
कातिक होत दिवाकर नेता ।।
अगहन भिन्न विष्णु हैं पूसहिं ।
पुरुष नाम रविहैं मलमासहिं ।।

***yama bhadom ashvina himareta*** |
***katika hota divakara neta*** ||
***agahana bhinna vishnu haim pusahim*** |
***purusha nama ravihaim malamasahim*** ||

**Meaning:** *Shri Surya Dev!* Thou melt snow and dispel chillness by riding your chariot with seven horses! As the creator of the day, you eliminate all unacceptable and harmful elements. During the Pusha month, you are referred to as the eagle-laden *Shri Maha-Vishnu*; during inauspicious months, for example, *Aashada* and *Agahana* (also called *Margasira*), you are described as *Ravi*.

We strongly advise consulting an experienced and expert Vedic astrologer for professional assessment of your horoscope and further guidance. Please watch YouTube videos for correct pronuciation of the Chalisa, mantras, chants etc.

## || दोहा || Concluding prayer

भानु चालीसा प्रेम युत, गावहिं जे नर नित्य,
सुख सम्पत्ति लहि बिबिध, होंहिं सदा कृतकृत्य।।

***bhanu chalisa prema yuta, gavahim je nara nitya,***
***sukha sampatti lahi bibidha, honhim sada kritakritya ||***

**Meaning:** *Shri Surya Dev!* Anyone who chants this *Bhanu Chalisa* with love and dedication every day will be granted happiness, money, and success in all their endeavors.

We strongly advise consulting an experienced and expert Vedic astrologer for professional assessment of your horoscope and further guidance. Please watch YouTube videos for correct pronuciation of the Chalisa, mantras, chants etc.

# Surya Dev Chalisa II

In Hindi and its English Transliteration

|| दोहा ||
|| Doha ||

श्री रविहरत आ होरात तमे, अगणित किरण पसारी,
वंदन करू टन चरण मे़ं, अर्घ देऊ जल धारी,

***Shri raviharat aa horat tame, aganit kiran pasari,***
***Vandan karu tan charan mein, argh devu jal dhari,***

सकल श्रीस्टी के स्वामी हो, सचराचर के नाथ,
निसदिन होत हे तुमसे ही, होवत संध्या प्रभात.

***Sakal shristi ke swami ho, sachrachar ke nath,***
***Nisdin hot he tumse hi, hovat sandhya prabhat.***

चौपाइ : **Chaupaai:**

जय भगवान सूर्य तुमहारी,
जय खगेश दिनकर सुभकारी,
तुम हो श्रिस्टी के नेत्रा स्वरूपा,
त्रिगुण धारी त्रै वेद स्वरूपा.

***Jai bhagwan surya tamhari,***
***jai khagesh dinkar subhkari,***
***Tum ho shristi ke netra swaroopa,***
***trigun dhari trai ved swaroopa.***

We strongly advise consulting an experienced and expert Vedic astrologer for professional assessment of your horoscope and further guidance. Please watch YouTube videos for correct pronuciation of the Chalisa, mantras, chants etc.

तुम ही करता पालक संहारक, भुवन चतुर्दश के संचालक,
सुन्दर वदन चतुर्भुज धारी, रश्मी रती तुम गगन विहारी,
चकरा शंख आरू स्वेट कमलधर, वरमुद्रा सोहत चोटेकार,
शीश मुकट कुंडल गाल माला, चारू तिलक तव भाल विशाला.

***Tum hi karta palak sanharak, bhuvan chaturdash ke sanchalak,***
***Sundar vadan chaturbhuj dhari, rashmi rathi tum gagan vihari,***
***Chakra shankh aru swet kamaldhar, varmudra sohat chothekar,***
***Shish mukat kundal gal mala, charu tilak tav bhal vishala.***

शाख्त अश्वा रात द्रुत गामी, अरुण सारथी गति अविरामी,
राख्त वरण आभुसन धारक, अतिप्रिया तोहे लाल पदारथ,
सर्वतमा काहे तुम्ही ऋग्वेदा, मेटरा काहे तुम को सब वेडा,
पांच देव मे़ं पूजे जाते, मन वंचित फल साधक पते.

***Shakht ashwa rat drut gami, arun sarathi gati avirami,***
***Rakht varan abhusan dharak, atipriya tohe lal padarath,***
***Sarvatama kahe tumhi rigveda, metra kahe tum ko sab veda,***
***Panch dev mein pooje jate, man vanchit phal sadhak pate.***

द्वादश नाम जाप आऔधरक, रोग शोक आरू कस्त निवारक,
मया कुन्ती तव ध्यान लगायो, दानवीर सूट कारण सो पायो,
राजा युधिस्ठिर तव जस गयो, अक्षय पटरा वो बन मे़ं पायो,
शास्त्रा त्याग अर्जुन अकुरयो, बन आदित्य ह्दय से पायो.

***Dwadash naam jaap aaudharak, rog shok aru kasth nivarak,***
***Maa kunti tav dhyan lagayo, danveer sut karan so payo,***
***Raja Yudhisthir tav jas gayo, akshay patra vo ban mein payo,***
***Shastra tyag arjun akurayo, ban aditya hriday se payo.***

We strongly advise consulting an experienced and expert Vedic astrologer for professional assessment of your horoscope and further guidance. Please watch YouTube videos for correct pronuciation of the Chalisa, mantras, chants etc.

विन्ध्याचल तब मार्ग में आयो, हाहा कर तिमिर से छायो,
मुनि अगस्त्य गिरि गर्व मीटायो, निजटक बन से विंध्या ना वयो,
मुनि अगस्तय तव महिमा गयी, सुमिर भये विजयी रघुराई,
तोहे विरोक मधुर फल जाना, मुख में लीन्ही तोहे हनुमाना.

***Vindyachal tab marg mein aayo, haha kar timir se chayo,***
***muni agastya giri garv mitayo, nijtak ban se vindhya na vayo,***
***muni agastay tav mahima gayi, sumir bhaye vijayi raghurai,***
***Tohe virok madhur phal jana, mukh mein linhi tohe hanumana.***

तव नंदन शनिदेव कहावे, पवन ते सूट शनी तीर मिटवे,
यज्ना व्रत स्तुति तुम्हारी किन्ही, भेट शुक्ला यगुर्वेद की दीन्ही,
सूर्यमुखी खरी तर तव रूपा, कृष्णा सुदर्शन भानु स्वरूपा,
नमन तोहे ओंकार स्वरूपा, नमन आत्मा आरू काल स्वरूपा.

***Tav nandan shanidev kahave, pavan te sut shani tir mitave,***
***Yagna vrat stuti tumhari kinhi, bhet shukla yagurved ki dinhi,***
***Suryamukhi khari tar tav roopa, krishna sudarshan bhanu swaroopa,***
***Naman tohe omkar swaroopa, naman aatma aru kaal swaroopa.***

डिग–दिगंत तव तेज प्रकाशे, उज्ज्वल रूप तुमहि आकाशे,
दस दिगपाल करत तव सुमिरन, आंजन नेत्रा करत हे सुमिरन,
त्रिविध टाप हारता तुम भगवान, ज्ञान ज्योति करता तुम भगवान,
सफल बनावे तव आराधन, गयत्री जाप साई हे साधन,

***Dig-digant tav tej prakashe, ujjwal roop tumahi aakashe,***
***Das digpal karat tav sumiran, aanjan netra karat he sumiran,***
***Trividh taap harta tum bhagwan, Gyan jyoti karta tum bhagwan,***
***Safal banave tav aaradhan, gayatri jaap sarh he sadhan,***

We strongly advise consulting an experienced and expert Vedic astrologer for professional assessment of your horoscope and further guidance. Please watch YouTube videos for correct pronuciation of the Chalisa, mantras, chants etc.

संध्या त्रिकल करत जो कोई, पावे कृपा सदा तव वोही,
चिईन्न शांती सूर्यशटक देवे, व्याधि उपाधी सब हर लेवे,
आस्ठदल कमल यंत्रा सुभकारी, पूजा उपसन तव सुखकारी,
माघ माज सुद्ध सप्तमी पवन, आरंभ हो तव सुभ व्रत पालन.

***Sandhya trikal karat jo koi, pave kripa sada tav wohi,***
***Chitt shanti suryashtak deve, vyadhi upadhi sab har leve,***
***Aasthdal kamal yantra subhkari, pooja upasan tav sukhkari,***
***Magh maas suddh saptami pavan, aarambh ho tav subh vrat palan.***

भानु सप्तमी मंगल करी, भक्ति दायिनी दोषं हरि,
रवि वासर जो तुम को ध्यावे, पुत्रादिक सुख वैभव पावे,
पाप रूपी पर्वत के विनाशी, वज्र रूप तुम हो अविनाशी,
राहू आन तव ग्रास बनावे, ग्रहण सूर्य तब को लग जाये.

***Bhanu saptami mangal kari, bhakti dayini doshan hari,***
***Ravi vasar jo tum ko dhyave, putradik sukh vaibhav pave,***
***Paap roopi parvat ke vinashi, vajr roop tum ho avinashi,***
***Rahu aan tav gras banave, grahan surya tab ko lag jaye.***

धर्म दान टाप करत है साधक, मिटत राहू तब पीड़ा बधक,
सूर्य देव तब कृपा कीजे, दीर्घा आयु बाल बुद्धि डेजे,
सूर्य उपासना कर नित ध्यावे, कुस्त रोग से मुक्ति पावे,
दक्षिण दिशा तोरी गति ग्यावे, दक्षिणायन वोही केहलावे.

***Dharm dan tap karat hai sadhak, mitat rahu tab pida badhak,***
***Surya dev tab kripa kije, dirgha aayu bal buddhi deje,***
***Surya upasana kar nit dhyave, kusth rog se mukti pave,***
***Dakshin disha tori gati gyave, dakshinayan wohi kehlave.***

We strongly advise consulting an experienced and expert Vedic astrologer for professional assessment of your horoscope and further guidance. Please watch YouTube videos for correct pronuciation of the Chalisa, mantras, chants etc.

उत्तर मार्जी तो उरु रथ होवे, उतरायण तब वो केहलावे,
मन आरू वचन कर्म हो पवन, संयम करत भले नित आर्धन.

***Uttar margi to uru rath hove, utrayan tab wo kehlave,***
***Man aru vachan karm ho pavan, sanyam karat bhale nit aardhan.***

|| दोहा ||

Doha

भारत दस चिंतन करत, धार दिन कर तव ध्यान,
रखियो कृपा इस भक्त पे, तुम्हारी सूर्य भगवान.

***Bharat das chintan karat, dhar din kar tav dhyan,***
***Rakhiyo kripa is bhakt pe, tumhari surya bhagwan.***

We strongly advise consulting an experienced and expert Vedic astrologer for professional assessment of your horoscope and further guidance. Please watch YouTube videos for correct pronuciation of the Chalisa, mantras, chants etc.

# CHAPTER 3

# Surya Dev Ji ki Aarti

## Surya Dev Ji ki Aarti (I)

The most well-known *Aarti* of *Surya Dev* is ***Jai Kashyap Nandan*** and is recited on *Surya Dev* related occasions.

जय कश्यप–नन्दन, ॐ जय अदिति नन्दन।
***Jai Kashyap-Nandan, Om Jai Aditi-Nandan*** |

त्रिभुवन – तिमिर – निकन्दन, भक्त – हृदय – चन्दन।।
***Tribhuvana-Timira-Nikandana,***
***Bhakta-Hridaya-Chandana***||

जय कश्यप–नन्दन, ॐ जय अदिति नन्दन।
***Jai Kashyap-Nandan, Om Jai Aditi-Nandan***|

सप्त–अश्वरथ राजित, एक चक्रधारी।
***Sapta-Ashvaratha Rajita, Ek Chakradhari***|

We strongly advise consulting an experienced and expert Vedic astrologer for professional assessment of your horoscope and further guidance. Please watch YouTube videos for correct pronuciation of the Chalisa, mantras, chants etc.

दुःखहारी, सुखकारी, मानस–मल–हारी।।
***Dukhahari- Sukhakari, Manasa-Mala-Hari***||

जय कश्यप–नन्दन, ॐ जय अदिति नन्दन।
***Jai Kashyap-Nandan, Om Jai Aditi-Nandan***|

सुर – मुनि – भूसुर – वन्दित,विमल विभवशाली।
***Sura-Muni-Bhusura-Vandita, Vimala Vibhavashali***|

अघ–दल–दलन दिवाकर,दिव्य किरण माली।।
***Agha-Dala-Dalana Diwakara, Divya Kirana Mali***||

जय कश्यप–नन्दन, ॐ जय अदिति नन्दन।
***Jai Kashyap-Nandan, Om Jai Aditi-Nandan***|

सकल – सुकर्म – प्रसविता,सविता शुभकारी।
***Sakala-Sukarma-Prasavita, Savita Shubhakari***|

विश्व–विलोचन मोचन, भव–बन्धन भारी।।
***Vishwa-Vilochana Mochana, Bhava Bandhana Bhari***||

जय कश्यप–नन्दन, ॐ जय अदिति नन्दन।
***Jai Kashyap-Nandan, Om Jai Aditi-Nandan***|

कमल–समूह विकासक,नाशक त्रय तापा।
***Kamala-Samuha-Vikasaka, Nashaka Traya Tapa***|

सेवत साहज हरतअति मनसिज–संतापा।।
***Sevata Sahaja Harata, Ati Manasija-Santapa***||

जय कश्यप – नन्दन, ॐ जय अदिति नन्दन।
***Jai Kashyap-Nandan, Om Jai Aditi-Nandan|***

नेत्र–व्याधि हर सुरवर, भू–पीड़ा–हारी।
***Netra-Vyadhi-Hara Survara Bhu-Pida-Hari|***

वृष्टि विमोचन संतत,परहित व्रतधारी।।
***Vrishti-Vimochana Santata Parahita-Vratadhari||***

जय कश्यप–नन्दन, ॐ जय अदिति नन्दन।
***Jai Kashyap-Nandan, Om Jai Aditi-Nandan|***

सूर्यदेव करुणाकर, अब करुणा कीजै।
***Suryadeva Karunakara, Ab Karuna Kijai|***

हर अज्ञान–मोह सब, तत्वज्ञान दीजै।।
***Hara Agyana-Moha Sab Tatvagyana Dijai||***

जय कश्यप–नन्दन, ॐ जय अदिति नन्दन।
***Jai Kashyap-Nandan, Om Jai Aditi-Nandan|***

We strongly advise consulting an experienced and expert Vedic astrologer for professional assessment of your horoscope and further guidance. Please watch YouTube videos for correct pronuciation of the Chalisa, mantras, chants etc.

# Surya Dev Ji ki Aarti (II)

ॐ जय सूर्य भगवान। जय हो तिनकर भगवान।
जगत के नेत्र स्वरूपा। तुम हो त्रिगुणा स्वरूपा।
धरता सबही सब ध्यान ।।
ॐ जय सूर्य भगवान...

***Om Jai Surya Bhagwan | Jai Ho Tinkar Bhagwan |***
***Jagat Ke Netra Swaroopa | Tum Ho Triguna Swaroopa |***
***Dharata Sabahi Sab Dhyan ||***
***Om Jai Surya Bhagwan...***

सारथी अरुण है प्रभु तुम। श्वेता कमालाधारी।
तुम चार भुजा धारी। अश्वा है साथ तुम्हारे।
कोटि किराना पसारे। तुम हो देव महान।।
ॐ जय सूर्य भगवान....

***Sarathi Arun Hai Prabhu Tum | Shweta Kama|adhari |***
***Tum Char Bhuja Dhari | Ashwa Hai Saath Tumharey |***
***Koti Kirana Pasaarey | Tum Ho Dev Mahan ||***
***Om Jai Surya Bhagwan....***

उषा काल में जब तुम। उदय चल आते।
तब सब दर्शन पाते। फैलाते उजीआरा।
जागता तब जग सारा। करे तब सब गुण गान।।
ॐ जय सूर्य भगवान....

***Usha Kaa| Mein Jab Tum | Udaya Chal Aatey |***
***Tab Sab Darshan Paatey | Phailaatey Ujiaara |***
***Jaagta Tab Jag Saara | Karey Tab Sab Gun Gaan ||***
***Om Jai Surya Bhagwan....***

We strongly advise consulting an experienced and expert Vedic astrologer for professional assessment of your horoscope and further guidance. Please watch YouTube videos for correct pronuciation of the Chalisa, mantras, chants etc.

भूचर जलचार खेचार। सब के हो प्राण तुम्ही।
सब जीवो के प्राण तुम्ही। वेद पुराण भखाने।
धर्म सभी तुम्हे माने। तुम ही सर्व शक्तिमान।।
ॐ जय सूर्य भगवान....

***Bhoochar Ja|char Khechar | Sab Ke Ho Pran Tumhi |***
***Sab Jeevo Ke Pran Tumhi | Ved Puraan Bhakhaaney |***
***Dharm Sabhi Tumhe Maaney | Tum Hi Sarva Shaktimaan ||***
***Om Jai Surya Bhagwan….***

पूजन करती विशाएं। पूजे सब एक पार।
तुम भुवनो के प्रतिपाल। ऋतुएं तुम्हारी दासी।
तुम शशक अविनाशी, शुभकारी अंशुमान।।
ॐ जय सूर्य भगवान....

***Pujan Karti Vishayein | Pujey Sab Ek Paar |***
***Tum Bhuvno Ke Pratipaal | Rituyein Tumhari Daasi |***
***Tum Shashaka Avinashi | Shubhkari Anshumaan ||***
***Om Jai Surya Bhagwan….***

We strongly advise consulting an experienced and expert Vedic astrologer for professional assessment of your horoscope and further guidance. Please watch YouTube videos for correct pronuciation of the Chalisa, mantras, chants etc.

## Surya Dev Ji ki Aarti (III)

जय जय जय रविदेव जय जय जय रविदेव।

***Jai Jai Jai Ravidev Jai Jai Jai Ravidev*** |

रजनीपति मदहारी शतलद जीवन दाता।।

***Rajanipati Madhaari Shat|ad Jeevan Daata*** ||

पटपद मन मदुकारी हे दिनमण दाता।

***Patpad Mann Madukaari Hey Dinmann Daataa*** |

जग के हे रविदेव जय जय जय स्वदेव।।

***Jag Ke He Ravidev Jai Jai Jai Swadev*** ||

नभ मंडल के वाणी ज्योति प्रकाशक देवा।

***Nabh Manda| Ke Vaani yoti Prakaashak Deva*** |

निजजन हित सुखराशी तेरी हम सब सेवा।।

***Nijjan Hit Sukhraashi Teri Hum Sab Sevaa*** ||

करते हैं रविदेव जय जय जय रविदेव।

***Karte Hai Ravi Dev Jai Jai Jai Ravidev*** |

कनक बदन मन मोहित रुचिर प्रभा प्यारी।।

***Kanak Badan Man Mohit Ruchir Prabha Pyari*** ||

We strongly advise consulting an experienced and expert Vedic astrologer for professional assessment of your horoscope and further guidance. Please watch YouTube videos for correct pronuciation of the Chalisa, mantras, chants etc.

नित मंडल से मंडित अजर अमर छविधारी।

***Nit Mandal Se Mandit Ajar Amar Chavidhaari |***

हे सुरवर रविदेव जय जय जय रविदेव।।

***Hey Survar Ravidev Jai Jai Jai Ravidev, ||***

We strongly advise consulting an experienced and expert Vedic astrologer for professional assessment of your horoscope and further guidance. Please watch YouTube videos for correct pronuciation of the Chalisa, mantras, chants etc.

# CHAPTER 4

# Surya Mantras

When recited with devotion, faith, and emotion, a mantra combines divine words or sounds that invoke the attention of the relevant God, Goddess, or deity and secures their heavenly blessings. When a person regularly begins chanting Mantras related to a specific deity, the distance between him and the concerned divine force gradually narrows. The regular use of *mantra* forms a subtle link, and one can obtain any desired boon within the deity's power. Wealth, prosperity, fame, fearlessness, success, and spiritual upliftment can all be obtained. To reap the most benefits from mantras and chanting, we must chant mantras daily to keep our energy levels high.

For the optimal benefits, any *Surya Mantra* should be recited 7000 times, and the chanting should be completed in 43 days, according to *Vedic* Astrology.

We strongly advise consulting an experienced and expert Vedic astrologer for professional assessment of your horoscope and further guidance. Please watch YouTube videos for correct pronuciation of the Chalisa, mantras, chants etc.

How to Recite/Chant the *Surya Mantra*

- You are free to choose any *Surya mantra* from this list.
- Try commencing the chanting of the *Surya mantras* on Sundays, as these are the most auspicious days for *Surya Dev* worship.
- Preferably initiate the chanting of the *mantras* in the waxing phase of the moon which is known as during *Shukla Paksha* in *Vedic* scripts.
- Always (if possible) start the prayers before daybreak/ sunrise.
- Sit on a red cloth with your back to the Sun God
- Light an earthen *diya* (lamp) with cow *ghee.*
- In your *puja* room, place a picture of *Surya Dev* or the *Surya Yantra* in front of you.
- Lord *Ganesh*, Lord *Vishnu*, Lord *Shiva*, and Lord *Surya* are all deities to be worshiped.
- Begin the chanting by reciting the *mantras* 108 times.
- To be open to receive the beneficial vibrations that arise from chanting the *Surya Mantras*, your mind must be rid of all negative thoughts.
- When the chanting is finished, offer Lord *Surya* water in a copper utensil.
- The *Surya Mantra* should be chanted at *Brahma Muhurta* or prior to sunrise.
- You can also offer wheat, as wheat is the Sun God's favorite grain. Red-colored flowers, such as red lotus or red hibiscus, can also be offered to *Surya Dev's* picture.
- When chanting the *Surya Mantra*, it is best to use a *Jaap mala* (rosary) made of transparent quartz crystal or red coral.

We strongly advise consulting an experienced and expert Vedic astrologer for professional assessment of your horoscope and further guidance. Please watch YouTube videos for correct pronuciation of the Chalisa, mantras, chants etc.

When you chant *Surya Mantra* regularly, you will notice the following benefits:

- The *Surya mantra* increases your energy level and you feel charged up and energized.
- You gain wealth and your overall health begins to improve.
- *Surya Mantra* helps your vision and has the power to cure your eye diseases, if any.
- The divine grace of the Sun God shields you from your enemies.
- The *Surya Mantra* bestows knowledge as well as the ability to work quickly.
- Physical and mental endurance is increasing and it makes you brave and heroic.
- You start to believe that you can easily overcome all of life's challenges.
- You become more charitable and imbibe higher moral standards.
- All negative thoughts, such as anger, ego, greed, jealousy, and betrayal, are cleansed from your mind.

These *Surya mantras* are incredibly potent and provide the desired outcomes if appropriately recited. It would be best if you recite the *Surya Mantra* according to the recommended methodology for the desired outcomes.

## Surya Namaskar Mantra

The *Surya Namaskara* is done before sunrise. *Mantras* are recited to pray to *Surya Dev*, and flowers, and rice grains are offered with water to the God. There are 12 *mantras*, each of which is a different name for the Sun God. A different *mantra* is chanted with each posture.

*Surya Namaskar Mantras* are as follows:

1. ***"Aum Mitraya Namah"*** means salutation to one who is friendly to all.
2. ***"Aum Ravayre Namah"*** means salutation to the shining one, the radiant one.
3. ***"Aum Suryaya Namah"*** means salutation to the one who is the dispeller of darkness.
4. ***"Aum Bhanave Namah"*** means salutation to the one who light up, the bright one.
5. ***"Aum Khagaya Namah"*** means salutation to the one who is all-pervading, one who moves through the sky.
6. ***"Aum Pushne Namah"*** means salutation to the giver of nourishment and fulfillment.
7. ***"Aum Hiranyagarbhaya Namah"*** means salutation to the one who has golden brilliance.
8. ***"Aum Marichaye Namah"*** means salutation to the giver of light with infinite rays.
9. ***"Aum Adityaya Namah"*** means salutation to the son of Aditi, the cosmic divine Mother.
10. ***"Aum Savitre Namah"*** means salutation to the one who is responsible for life.

We strongly advise consulting an experienced and expert Vedic astrologer for professional assessment of your horoscope and further guidance. Please watch YouTube videos for correct pronuciation of the Chalisa, mantras, chants etc.

11. ***"Aum Arkaya Namah"*** means salutation to the one worthy of praise and glory.
12. ***"Aum Bhaskaraya Namah"*** means salutation to the giver of wisdom and cosmic brilliance.

## Surya Beej Mantra

Positive energy and grace from the *Surya Dev* are provided through the recitation of the potent *Beej Mantra*.

With the help of this potent *Surya Beej mantra*, you can connect with *Surya Dev's* (Sun's) higher frequencies. One receives his divine favor in the form of excellent health, wealth, and fame. For optimal effects, begin reciting this *Surya Beej mantra* on Sunday and continue for 41 days.

ॐ हराम हरिम ह्रौं सह सूर्याय नमः

***"Om Hraam Hreem Hraum Sah Suryay Namah"***

**Meaning:** 'I salute the Great Sun God for his Divine grace.'

The Surya Beej mantra can bring about a life of fame, fortune, and austerity. It also can heal illnesses and any other adverse effects.

We strongly advise consulting an experienced and expert Vedic astrologer for professional assessment of your horoscope and further guidance. Please watch YouTube videos for correct pronuciation of the Chalisa, mantras, chants etc.

## Surya Gayatri Mantra

*Surya Gayatri Mantra* first appeared in the *Rig Veda* (the ancient Hindu sacred scriptures and hymns written in the Vedic language during the Vedic period). This supreme mantra addresses the Sun God (*Surya Dev*) and is widely regarded as one of Hinduism's oldest and most powerful mantras. The *Surya Gayatri Mantra* praises the Sun and invokes its positive energy and divine blessings. The mantra affects all three aspects of your being. It improves your physical health, mental clarity, and spiritual well-being.

First, take your morning bath and dress in white clothing. It would be best if you filled a copper pot with water and added some *ashtagandha*, rice, and red flowers. Offer this water to Sun (*Surya Dev*). Sit on a woolen sheet in front of the Lord and chant this mantra with your 108-bead *tulsi* (basil) rosary.

Sunday is the best day to start chanting.

ॐ आदित्याय विद्महे मार्त्तण्डाय धीमहि तन्नः सूर्यः प्रचोदयात् ।।

***"Om Adityaya Vidmahe Sahasra Kiranaya Dhimahi Tanno Surya Prachodayaat"***

ॐ भास्कराय विद्महे महादुत्याथिकराया
धीमहि तनमो आदित्य प्रचोदयात् ।।

***"Om Bhaskaray Vidmahe Martanday Dheemahi Tanah Surya Prachodayat"***

We strongly advise consulting an experienced and expert Vedic astrologer for professional assessment of your horoscope and further guidance. Please watch YouTube videos for correct pronuciation of the Chalisa, mantras, chants etc.

**Meaning:** 'Om, allow me to meditate on the Sun God, Oh, maker of the day, give me superior intellect, and let Sun God illuminate my mind.'

Begin reciting the *Surya Gayatri Mantra* at sunrise or during the day's *Brahma Muhurta* or *Surya Hora*. Start by meditating four times on the *Surya mantra* every Sunday during *Shukla Paksha*, *Sapthami Thithi*, *Makar Sankranti*, or *Rakha Sapthami*.

If you cannot chant the *Surya Gayatri mantras* regularly, recite them on Sundays and *Sapthami Thithi*. Worship *Surya Dev* with incense and flowers and perform one rosary of this *mantra* facing east. Continue to fast on Sunday for better results in life.

This liberating *mantra* generates positive energy and divine benefits from the Sun God when sung daily with complete concentration in adoration of the Sun God. It improves physical health, mental clarity, and spiritual well-being. One can get popularity and success wherever and anywhere by reciting the mantra.

## Other Surya Gayatri Mantras

ॐ सप्त–तुरंगाय विद्महे सहस्र–किरणाय धीमहि तन्नो रविः प्रचोदयात् ।।

***Om Sapt Turangay Vidhmahe Sahasra Kirnay Dheemahi Tanno Ravi Prachodyat* ||**

ॐ अश्वाद्वाजय विद्महे पासहस्थाया धीमहि तन्नो सूर्य प्रचोदयात ।।

***Om Aswadwajaya Vidhmahe Pasa Hasthaya Dheemahi ! Tanno Surya Prachodayat !***

ॐ भास्कराय विधमहे दिवा कराय धीमहि तन्नो सूर्य प्रचोदयात ।।

***Om Bhaskaraya Vidhmahe Diva karaya Dheemahe Thanno Surya Prachodayath* ||**

ॐ आस्वादवजया विधमहे पासा हस्ताय धीमहि तन्नो सूर्य प्रचोदयात ।।

***Om Aswadwajaya Vidhmahe Pasa Hasthaya Dheemahe Thanno Surya Prachodayath* ||**

ॐ आदित्याय विद्महे मार्त्तण्डाय धीमहि तन्नः सूर्यः प्रचोदयात ।।

***Om Aadityay Vidhmahe Martanday Dheemahi Tanah: Surya: Prachodyat* ||**

We strongly advise consulting an experienced and expert Vedic astrologer for professional assessment of your horoscope and further guidance. Please watch YouTube videos for correct pronuciation of the Chalisa, mantras, chants etc.

## Surya Gayatri Mantra in Gujarati

ઑં અશ્વટ્વજાય વડ્મિહે
પાસ હસ્થાયૈ ધીમહિ
થણ્નો સૂર્ય પ્રછોદયાઠ્

## Surya Gayatri Mantra in Telugu

ఓం అశ్వట్వజాయ విట్మహే
పాస హస్థయ ధీమహి
ధణ్నో సూర్య ప్రఛోదయాత్

## Surya Gayatri Mantra in Kannada

ಓಂ ಅಶವಥವಜಾಯ◌ೈ ಪಿಟಿಮಹ◌ೀ
ಪಾಸ ಹಸತಾಯ◌ೈ ಧ◌ೀಮಹೆ
ತನನ◌ೋ ಸೂರಯ ಪರಚ◌ೋದಯಾತ

## Surya Gayatri Mantra in Tamil

ஓம் அஷ்வத்வஜாய வித்மஹே
பாச ஹஸ்தாய தீமஹி
தந்நே◌ா சூர்ய ப்ரசே◌ாதயாத்

## Surya Gayatri Mantra in Malayalam

ഓം അശ്വത്വജായൈ വിദ്മഹേ
പാസ ഹസ്തായൈ ധീമഹി
തണ്നേ◌ാ സൂര്യ പ്രചേ◌ാദയാത്

We strongly advise consulting an experienced and expert Vedic astrologer for professional assessment of your horoscope and further guidance. Please watch YouTube videos for correct pronuciation of the Chalisa, mantras, chants etc.

## Surya Mantra

**This *mantra* can be chanted to bask in the divine grace of the Sun God. It is known to eradicate diseases from their roots and aid in developing the physical and mental endurance required to overcome all of life's challenges.**

नमः सूर्याय शान्ताय सर्वरोग निवारिणे
आयु ररोग्य मैस्वैर्यं देहि देवः जगत्पते।।

***"Namah Suryaya Shantaya Sarvaroga Nivaarine***
***Ayu rarogya maisvairyam dehi devah jagatpate"***

**Meaning:** 'O! Lord Surya, ruler of the universe, you are the remover of all diseases, the source of peace. I bow to you and please bless your devotees with long life, health, and wealth.'

We strongly advise consulting an experienced and expert Vedic astrologer for professional assessment of your horoscope and further guidance. Please watch YouTube videos for correct pronuciation of the Chalisa, mantras, chants etc.

# Aditya Hrudhayam Mantra

'*Hridaya*' refers to anything particularly nourishing and healing for heart. The one who shines or resides in the heart is referred to as *hridayam*.

When one recites this *mantra*, the Sun's light bestows knowledge and the ability to work quickly. When used to invoke the Sun God, this chant makes one brave and frees them from negative emotions such as ego, rage, greed, want, and betrayal.

आधित्य ह्रुधाय पुण्यं सर्व सथृ विनासनं
जयावहं जबे नित्यं अक्षयं परमं शिवं

***"Aadhitya Hrudhaya Punyam Sarva Sathru Vinaasanam***
***Jayaavaham Jabe nithyam Akshayam Paramam Shivam*** ||"

**Meaning:** This mantra can be used to express gratitude to Surya Dev.

Chanting the *Surya Mantras* can help one start on the path to discovering their inner beauty and power. The regular recitation of this mantra satisfies devotees' worldly desires.

*Surya's* various qualities, such as self-discipline, reputation, general vigor, courage, and authority, are brought into one's daily life through these mantras. However, prescribed rules must be followed while chanting to achieve the best results.

We strongly advise consulting an experienced and expert Vedic astrologer for professional assessment of your horoscope and further guidance. Please watch YouTube videos for correct pronuciation of the Chalisa, mantras, chants etc.

## Surya Vashikaran Mantra

ॐ नमो भगवते श्री–सूर्याय ह्रीं सहस्त्र–किरणाय ऐं
अतुल–बल–पराईद्रमाय नव–ग्रह–दश–दिक–पाल–लक्ष्मी–देव–वाय,
धर्म–कर्म–सहितायै 'अमुक' नाथय नाथय,
मोहय मोहय, आकर्षय आकर्षय,
दासानुदासं कुरु–कुरु, वश कुरु–कुरु स्वाहा।।

***Om Namoh Bhagawate Shree-Suryay***
***Hreem Sahashtra Kiranay Aim***
***Atul-Bal-Paraakramay Nava – Graha –***
***Dash – Dik – Paal – Lakṣhmi – Dev – Vay,***
***Dharma – Karma – Sahitayai 'Amuka' Nathay Nathay,***
***Mohay Mohay, Akarshay Akarṣhay,***
***Daasanudaasam Kuru – Kuru, Vash Kuru – Kuru Swaha*** ||

This *Vashikaran* mantra works for love relationships and married life problems and is simple to use without complicated rituals. However, this *mantra* always comes with long and powerful words. The *Surya Vashikaran Mantra* requires time to complete the goal, but it produces incredible results.

After bathing, recite this *Mantra* 108 times and offer *Surya Dev* water with jaggery. It is suggested that you replace the word 'AMUK' with the name of your desired person while chanting this *mantra*. You must complete this task nine days a row for the best results.

We strongly advise consulting an experienced and expert Vedic astrologer for professional assessment of your horoscope and further guidance. Please watch YouTube videos for correct pronuciation of the Chalisa, mantras, chants etc.

# CHAPTER 5

# Ravivar (Sunday) Vrat (Fasting) Katha (Story)

There was once an elderly lady. She would take her bath first thing in the morning. She kept her house clean by plastering it with cow dung and only ate after offering food to the Sun God first. She had a good life. This lady used to go to her neighbor's house and collect cow dung. Her neighbor's wife was envious. She tethered her cow inside the room, preventing the old lady from collecting the dung. And because she couldn't plaster her house with cow dung, she didn't cook. She didn't even give the idols food. She kept her fast going all day and slept on an empty stomach.

In her dream, the Sun God appeared to her. Why didn't you eat your meals? He inquired. Why didn't you offer the Idols food? The old lady said politely, and my neighbor refused to let me collect cow dung from her yard. I was unable to clean my home. I don't have a cow of my own. I am pleased with you, said the Sun God, because you fasted

We strongly advise consulting an experienced and expert Vedic astrologer for professional assessment of your horoscope and further guidance. Please watch YouTube videos for correct pronuciation of the Chalisa, mantras, chants etc.

on Sunday. Your worship has pleased me. I will present you with a lovely cow. The God vanished. The elderly lady blinked her eyes open. In her courtyard was an adorable cow with a calf. She was taken aback to see them. She had hay and water ready for them.

The neighbor's lady became envious of the old lady's cow when she saw it in her house. She also noticed that the cow's dung was gold, not regular dung. She replaced the gold dung with her cow's regular dung. She continued the substitution practice for several days. When the Sun God realized that the old lady was being duped by her neighbor, he unleashed a storm at sunset. The old lady tethered it inside her room to keep her cow safe. She was surprised, however, to discover that her cow had given her gold dung rather than ordinary dung. She could see right through her neighbor's ruse.

The neighbor's lady was always envious and devised a scheme to deprive her of the wonder cow. She approached the king and said, My Lord, a poor old lady in our neighborhood has a divine cow. The cow excretes gold dung. If this cow is with you, it will be fitting for your graciousness. She hid it in her bedroom so no one could even catch a glimpse. The king was avaricious. He instructed his courtier to "go immediately and bring the When the courtier arrived; the old lady was about to offer food to the Sun Gods' idol. He untied the rope from the peg and took the cow with him, leaving the lady sobbing in vain. That day, the elderly lady skipped her meals. She prayed to God for the cow's safe return. She was unable to sleep at night.

On the other hand, the king was overjoyed to have that divine cow. He had a dream that night, and the Sun God was

We strongly advise consulting an experienced and expert Vedic astrologer for professional assessment of your horoscope and further guidance. Please watch YouTube videos for correct pronuciation of the Chalisa, mantras, chants etc.

there and said, I offered this cow to the old lady as a token of my affection for her worship of me. This cow does not belong to you.

The king awoke and was severely shaken. He noticed that the entire palace was covered in cow dung. There was a foul odor in the air. The king sent for the old lady with honor in the morning. He gave the cow back to the old lady and gave her some money. Everyone was relieved when the neighbor's lady was properly punished. The king declared that if his subjects wanted their desires to be fulfilled, they should fast on Sundays. All of his people were now prosperous. They were never afflicted. They were never subjected to a natural disaster. Everyone had a good time.

### Method to follow Ravivar (Sunday) Vrat (fasting)

In Hinduism, all the seven days of the week are dedicated to a divine being. Fasting on a Sunday is considered highly beneficial. *Vrat* means fast and *katha* means story. Worshiping the Sun God (*Surya Dev*) on Sunday is supposed to bring contentment, affluence, wealth, and security from enemies. Observing a fast and listening to the *Vrat katha* (story to be read or heard on the day of fasting) fulfills a person's desires and one is bestowed with public admiration, fortune, fame, and good health.

This fast should be practiced in the following manner.

- Wear clean clothes in the morning after you've finished bathing.

- Keep your cool and remember the Sun God.
- After that, perform rituals to honor Lord Surya with scent and flowers.
- After worshiping, listen to the *Vrat Katha*.
- After listening to the *Vrat Katha*, perform aarti.
- After that, remembering the Sun God, offer *sattvic** food and fruits to the Sun by pouring water on it.
- Food and fruits should not be eaten more than once and should be eaten prior to sunset.

Things to avoid while observing the Sunday fasting

- Salty and oily foods should be avoided.
- Avoid consuming food after sunset.

*The sattvic diet emphasizes one of the three yogic qualities (*guna*) known as *sattva*. Foods that decrease the body's energy are classified as *tamasic*, while foods that increase the body's energy are classified as *rajasic*. In modern literature, a sattvic diet is also known as a yogic diet. *Sattvic* diets share *sattvic* qualities such as "pure, essential, natural, vital, energy-containing, clean, conscious, true, honest, wise". A *sattvic* diet can also demonstrate *Ahimsa*, the principle of not harming other living beings.

## CHAPTER 6

# Remedies for a Malefic Sun in your horoscope as per Vedic Astrology

The Sun is the father of our solar system, and all planets revolve around it. The Sun represents the power of light in the celestial sky, the earth's temperature, the power of presentation, and progress. His presence denotes "day," while his absence denotes "night."

Ancient Vedic text acknowledge that it produces favorable results when the Sun is transitioning through or is placed in Houses 1 to 5,8,9,11, and 12. The 6th, 7th, and 10th houses are considered inauspicious for Sun. As per Vedic astrology, the planets that are friendly to Sun are the Moon, Jupiter, and Mars, while Saturn, Venus, Rahu, and Ketu are not pleasant. The first house is the house of the Sun's exaltation, while the seventh house is the house of debilitation. Mars in the sixth house and Ketu in the first house cause the Sun to produce heavenly results. If the Sun is placed in an auspicious house of a person's horoscope, he will rise in power and position. When the Sun and Mercury align, much better results are predicted.

If placed in the first house, the Sun will cause serious health issues for the native. Whereas if Sun is in the chart's second house, it will negatively impact the family and its comforts. The affectee's sisters and daughters will suffer due to the Sun's placement in the 6th house, and he will face challenges in the comforts of their spouse in the 7th. In critical situations, the Sun of the 8th house will save the native's life. The Sun in the 9th house will destroy the forefathers' comforts and may deprive the native of their property. The Sun will harm the father if placed in the 10th house. If the native does not supplement Saturn's power by consuming liquor, meat, and eggs, the Sun in the 11th increases and multiplies his income by orders of magnitude. The Sun in the 12th house destroys the native's nighttime comforts and sleep.

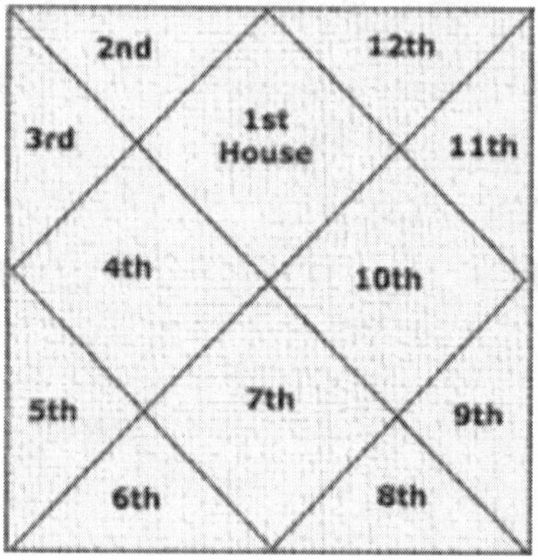


We strongly advise consulting an experienced and expert Vedic astrologer for professional assessment of your horoscope and further guidance. Please watch YouTube videos for correct pronuciation of the Chalisa, mantras, chants etc.

## INDICATIONS OF A WEAK SUN IN YOUR BIRTHCHART

It is strongly advised that an expert Vedic astrologer be consulted before attempting any remedies to ameliorate a malefic Sun in your horoscope,

Here are some signs of a weak Sun or a malevolent Sun:

- The individual is constantly self-conscious about their social standing and position.
- Due to a lack of self-confidence, such people are prone to develop narcissistic tendencies; they start singing their own praises.
- Such people have a strong sense of inferiority, which harms their social lives.
- Individuals lack drive and motivation and constantly seek assistance from others.
- In general, the native's father does not have a good fate.
- Natives with a weak Sun may also experience frequent limb numbness and physical problems.
- Some people may struggle because of poor vision, excessive salivation, or color blindness.

## REMEDIES FOR MALEFIC SUN, BASED ON PLACEMENT OF SUN IN BIRTHCHART

### Remedial Measures for a Weak/Inauspicious Sun in the 1st House

- Marry before reaching the age of 24.
- Avoid having sex with your spouse/partner during the day.

We strongly advise consulting an experienced and expert Vedic astrologer for professional assessment of your horoscope and further guidance. Please watch YouTube videos for correct pronuciation of the Chalisa, mantras, chants etc.

- Install a water pump in your ancestral home.
- Hammer a copper nail into each corner of your wooden bed posts.
- Make sure that your wealth is the result of your hard work.
- Build a small dark room on the left side of your house near the end.
- Avoid consumption of jaggery but your spouse must consume "*gur*," or jaggery.

**Remedial Measures for a Weak/Inauspicious Sun in the 2nd House**

- Provide religious institutions with donations of coconut, mustard oil, and almonds.
- Stay clear of confrontations regarding money, property, and women.
- Try to help other people without expecting anything in return.
- Try to fast on Sundays from sunrise to sundown if you can.
- On Sundays, offer water sweetened with jaggery to the Sun.
- Keep your persona pristine and impeccable.
- Ensure all your interactions with authorities and representatives are legal and ethical.
- Refrain from accepting donations, particularly of milk, silver, and rice.

We strongly advise consulting an experienced and expert Vedic astrologer for professional assessment of your horoscope and further guidance. Please watch YouTube videos for correct pronuciation of the Chalisa, mantras, chants etc.

## Remedial Measures for a Weak/Inauspicious Sun in the 3rd House

- Keep your mother and grandmother happy and seek their blessings.
- Give or donate milk or rice.
- Fast from sunrise to sunset on Sundays, if possible.
- On Sundays, offer water mixed with jaggery to the Sun.
- Be courteous to those around you.
- Listen to or read the *Harivansh Puran*.
- Adopt good morals and abstain from wrongdoing.

## Remedial Measures for a Weak/Inauspicious Sun in the 4th House

- Give food and alms to those who are in need.
- Consume no meat or alcohol.
- Do not engage in any illegal business or labor.
- *Aditya hrudayam stotram* can be read or listened to.
- Wear a gold or copper coin around your neck.
- Don't start a business associated with wood or iron.
- Businesses involving gold, silver, or textiles will generate excellent results.

## Remedial Measures for a Weak/Inauspicious Sun in the 5th House

- Build the kitchen is in the eastern section of your house.
- Avoid criticizing others unnecessarily
- Never lie to anyone
- Make sure you honor all your commitments

- Do not cover your home's verandah if you have one.
- Do not put off having a child.
- Drop a small amount of mustard oil on the ground every day for 43 days.

**Remedial Measures for a Weak/Inauspicious Sun in the 6th House**

- Keeping *Ganga Jal* (water from the holy river Ganges) in your home (in a silver utensil, if plausible) at all times is considered beneficial.
- Brown ants or alternatively monkeys can be fed wheat or *Gur* (jaggery).
- Ancestral customs and rituals must be strictly followed, otherwise the family progress and happiness may be jeopardized.
- If your father is ill, sleep with a glass of water next to your bed.
- Bury a square piece of copper in your home's yard.
- Hammer copper nails into the bedpost
- If possible, avoid building underground furnaces within the premises of a house.

**Remedial Measures for a Weak/Inauspicious Sun in the 7th House**

- Reduce your salt consumption.
- In your backyard, bury a square copper plate.
- On Sundays, fast.
- Maintain the cleanliness of your character.
- Hammer copper nails into the wooden bed posts.

We strongly advise consulting an experienced and expert Vedic astrologer for professional assessment of your horoscope and further guidance. Please watch YouTube videos for correct pronuciation of the Chalisa, mantras, chants etc.

- Begin any work after eating a small quantity of sweets (anything with sugar) and water.
- Raise, or serve a black or a hornless cow, but make sure it's not a white cow.

**Remedial Measures for a Weak/Inauspicious Sun in the 8th House**

- Before beginning any new task, always eat something sweet and drink water.
- Whenever possible, toss a few copper coins into a burning pyre (*Chita*).
- Avoid keeping a white cloth in the house.
- Never reside in a home that has a south-facing main door.
- Cast/float jaggery (*gur*) into the running water.
- Be honest and refrain from any wrong work.
- Be good to your elder brother.
- Listen to the *Harivansh Puran*.
- Keep a fast on Sundays.
- Do not steal.

**Remedial Measures for a Weak/Inauspicious Sun in the 9th House**

- Never accept silver or items made of silver as gifts or donations.
- Try and donate silver or things made of silver regularly.
- Try not to sell any brass family heirlooms that you may have in your possession.
- Avoid extremes of both rage/anger and tenderness/gentleness.

## Remedial Measures for a Weak/Inauspicious Sun in the 10th House

- If possible, avoid dressing in blue or black.
- Tossing a copper coin into a river or flowing water for 43 days will be highly beneficial.
- Avoid alcoholic beverages and non-vegetarian food.
- Try to avoid alcohol and maintain a vegetarian diet.
- Every day, pour water into a copper pot, decorate it with a red blossom, and sprinkle some *sindoor* on top and offer it to the rising Sun in the morning.
- Read the *Harivansh Puran* for yourself.

## Remedial Measures for a Weak/Inauspicious Sun in the 11th House

- Abstain from meat and alcohol.
- Keep some almonds close to the head and of your bed and offer them in the temple the following day.
- Get copper nails hammered into your bedposts.
- Avoid speaking lies.
- Donate wheat, jaggery, or copper.

## Remedial Measures for a Weak/Inauspicious Sun in the 12th House

- Observe fasts on Sundays.
- Every morning, within the first hour of sunrise, offer water to the Sun.
- One should be religious and honest and never give false testimony.

- Do not engage in business with your brother-in-law or uncles.
- Always forgive your adversaries/enemies and forgive those who do wrong to you.
- Do not accept any electrical articles for free.
- Try building a courtyard in your home or staying in a house that has a courtyard
- Keep a *chakki* (stone mill) in the house if possible.
- You must read the *Harivansh Puran*.

We strongly advise consulting an experienced and expert Vedic astrologer for professional assessment of your horoscope and further guidance. Please watch YouTube videos for correct pronuciation of the Chalisa, mantras, chants etc.

CHAPTER 7

# Remedies to energize Sun in your Horoscope

As per *Vedic* astrology, Sun travels from one zodiac sign to the next in nearly 30 days. Sun is considered the natural representative of the *Atman* (Soul), Father, and Government. When placed in its exalted sign Aries, it becomes strong; whereas when placed in Libra (its debilitated sign), it becomes weak. Sun governs the Leo (zodiac sign) and the Bile in your body.

Every planet has a profound impact on your life. The planet and its associated objects surround you whenever a planet's unique phase begins or transits through a specific house in your horoscope. This causes you to come under the influence of that planet. Every planet represents a different color and influences human life in various ways. Thus, to live a happy life, one should utilize (if a planet is benefic to you) or avoid (if a planet is malefic to you) specific things related to the planet in question.

We strongly advise consulting an experienced and expert Vedic astrologer for professional assessment of your horoscope and further guidance. Please watch YouTube videos for correct pronuciation of the Chalisa, mantras, chants etc.

Remedial measures always assist you in overcoming most of your worries and issues in various aspects of your life. We are attempting to tell you the most straightforward and best remedies to make the Sun stronger in your birth chart so that you can carry them out quickly and bring positive changes into your life.

## ENERGIZE SUN BY MAKING SOME CHANGES IN YOUR LIFESTYLE

- Try to dress up in red and saffron-colored clothing.
- You should respect your father, the government, and higher-ranking officials.
- You ought to get up early (before sunrise) and look at the rising sun with your own eyes, and it would fill you with zeal and optimistic energy.
- Every day, at sunrise, for about 10-15 minutes, stand facing the Sun with a smile, your eyes closed, and seek *Surya Dev's* blessings.

## ENERGIZE SUN BY OFFERING WATER TO SUN

- Offer water to the Sun every morning, if possible, within the first hour of sunrise.
- In a copper vessel *(lota)*, add a small red flower, a pinch of vermilion *(sindoor)*, and a few grains of rice, and fill it with water.
- **Method:** Standing in front of the Sun, raise the copper vessel of water above your head and pour forward,

We strongly advise consulting an experienced and expert Vedic astrologer for professional assessment of your horoscope and further guidance. Please watch YouTube videos for correct pronuciation of the Chalisa, mantras, chants etc.

ensuring that the Sun›s rays pass through the water before falling on you. Chant the Gayatri Mantra three times while pouring the water.

- One can also do this on cloudy days by facing in the direction you believe the Sun will be at that time, raising the copper vessel above your head, and beginning pouring.

## ENERGIZE SUN BY USING PRAYERS AS REMEDIES

- Prayers are the most effective way to connect your soul to the Almighty.
- Prayer requests that God to heal you, keep your morale high, and give you the strength to overcome any kind of challenge in your life.
- You gain hope and the power to carry out your actions with sincerity when you pray.
- You should worship *Surya Dev* or Lord *Vishnu* every day and recite *Aditya Hridaya Stotra* or *Harivansh Puran* to obtain the blessings of *Surya Dev*.
- Aside from that, you can also worship Lord *Shri Ram*, who is considered as the *Maha Vishnu's avatar*.

## ENERGIZE SUN BY FASTING ON SUNDAYS

- If plausible, you should fast on Sundays.
- Fasting is an authentic and sacred method to make *Surya Dev* happy.

- It is a process to detoxify your internal and external body and, at the same time, be able to devote yourself to the all-powerful entity.
- You gain willpower via fasting, which is beneficial in many ways.

## ENERGIZE SUN BY INDULGING IN CHARITY AND DONATIONS

- According to Vedic Astrology, the best way to get rid of the malefic effects of any planet is to indulge in charity and donations. This should be done with complete faith and devotion, with no expectation of compensation.
- Donations must go to someone deserving, needy, and suitable.
- Donations to the *Surya Dev* (Sun) should be made on Sunday, in *Sun's Hora*, and in *Sun's Nakshatra (Krittika, Uttara Phalguni, Uttara Ashadha*) before 8 a.m.
- Donate Jaggery, Wheat grains, Copper, Ruby gemstone, Red Flowers, and other home remedies to strengthen *Surya Dev* (Sun).
- Sun can also be energized by providing medicines to the ones in need.

## ENERGIZE SUN BY RECITING MANTRAS

- Since ancient times, mantras have held great significance in *Vedic* Astrology. Every mantra has a unique vibration and energizes a person with the powerful energy of a deity associated with that planet.

We strongly advise consulting an experienced and expert Vedic astrologer for professional assessment of your horoscope and further guidance. Please watch YouTube videos for correct pronuciation of the Chalisa, mantras, chants etc.

- *Surya Mantra* chanting is an excellent and straightforward way to appease *Surya Dev*; however, proper pronunciation is required. Aside from that, it would be best if you chanted a mantra up to a certain number of times to achieve the ultimate state.
- To appease Planet Sun, recite the Sun Beej Mantra (i.e.

***Aum Hraam Hreem Hraum Sah Suryaya Namah***

- It would be beneficial if you repeated this mantra 7000 times. According to *Desh-Kaal-Patra Siddhanta*, the Sun *Beej Mantra* should be chanted 4 times of 7000 in *Kalyuga*, so you should chant it 28000 times.
- You can also recite another *mantra,* i.e.

***Om Ghrini Suryay Namah***

## ENERGIZE SUN BY WEARING A RUDRAKSHA

- Lord Shiva's tears that fell on earth are known as *Rudraksha*. Each planet has unique characteristics, so each is represented by its unique *Rudraksha*. They are considered incredibly potent and used for spiritual upliftment in Vedic astrology. It is believed to bring prosperity, peace, and good health and aids in resolving problems in all walks of life. When you wear it, the divine grace of Lord *Shiva* is bestowed upon you.
- Wear 1 or 12 *Mukhi Rudraksha* while reciting a specific *Rudraksha* bead *mantra* for Planet Sun.

Mantra for wearing 1 *Mukhi Rudraksha*:

***Aum Hreem Namah***

OR

***Aum Yem Ham Shroum Ye***

Mantra for wearing 12 *Mukhi Rudraksha*:

***Aum Krom Shrom Roum Namah***

OR

***Aum Hrim Shrim Ghrini Shrim***

## ENERGIZE SUN BY WEARING A GEMSTONE

- As per Vedic astrology, Gemstones are significant in remedial measures to improve a malefic planet in your horoscope. These are commonly referred to as Gemstones or Birthstones and can be precious or semi-precious.
- Our divine earth is blessed with abundant mineral resources; these minerals and crystals have enigmatic healing properties and spiritual meanings. Every planet, when combined with a specific gemstone, aids in balancing that planet's effect on us.
- Wear a ring with natural Ruby on your ring finger starting any on Sunday before

We strongly advise consulting an experienced and expert Vedic astrologer for professional assessment of your horoscope and further guidance. Please watch YouTube videos for correct pronuciation of the Chalisa, mantras, chants etc.

- Perform this ritual before 8 a.m., during the Sun's *Hora*, or when *Sun's Nakshatra* in the brighter fortnight of the Lunar Month.
  - *The Hora is the time in a day that is ruled by a specific planet (the time between sunrise and sunset is divided into 12 equal parts). There are 24 Horas in a week, each ruled by a different planet, and they are present from dawn to sunset every day. The Horas are either beneficial or unfavorable for various vocations depending on the reigning planet. The Sun's Hora is lucky for all political work, interactions with and meetings with politicians, leaders, and government officials, job applications, interactions with the court, transactions involving money, buying, and selling, and risk-taking activities.*

## ENERGIZE SUN BY ESTABLISHMENT OF A YANTRA

- *Yantras*, like *Mantras*, are popular remedies in Vedic astrology. Yantras are typically drawn on *Bhojpatra* (parchment) and worn as a body talisman.
- It can be engraved on an amulet or pendant if you cannot make it. According to Vedic Astrology, there are nine planets, each with its own yantra. These Yantras are referred to as the *Navgrah yantra*.

- Below is how one can draw a *Surya Yantra*

| | | |
|---|---|---|
| 6 | 1 | 8 |
| 7 | 5 | 3 |
| 2 | 9 | 4 |

- *Yantras* are symmetrical diagrams that are used to supplement the efficacy of *mantras* and are supposed to be extremely beneficial in the following situations:
  - When one is unable to recite the Mantra for some reason,
  - Where the presence of a deity manifested as a symbol is required,
  - In cases where a native cannot afford the cost of gemstones.

## MISCELLANEOUS REMEDIES TO ENERGIZE AN INAUSPICIOUS SUN IN YOUR BIRTH CHART

Aside from the remedies listed above, you can perform the following to appease *Surya Dev* (Sun God) and reap its numerous benefits:

- Preferably *Surya Namaskar* should be done daily.
- Drink fenugreek tea: A teaspoon of fenugreek seeds is needed to make a cup of fenugreek tea. To taste, you can add a little honey. In addition to many other health benefits, this tea will help strengthen the Sun, Moon, and

Mars in your horoscope. Drink 1 to 2 cups of fenugreek tea per day. Drinking it during the Sun's hora will be even more beneficial.

- Allow water to sit in a copper vessel overnight, if possible, then drink from it first thing in the morning. This will strengthen the Sun in your birth chart and is an effective treatment for the body's poor sun-related disorders.
- Always show respect to your father or a father figure.
- Consumption of a handful of almonds (before sunset) is more than enough to strengthen the Sun's position in your body and in your astrological chart.
- Casting a copper coin into a river or canal for 43 days is extremely beneficial. Immersing a thing into the flowing water symbolizes submerging sorrows and miseries in the water and letting them flow away from you.
- Water the *Shwetark* tree (Scientific name: Calotropis gigantean) and nurture it as long as you possibly can.
- Gazing at the Sun and its red glow with naked eyes at sunrise is also a potent remedy.
- People with a weak Sun in their horoscope should drink a glass of water with sugar before starting any new project.
- Another excellent remedy is to stay away from eating meat as much as possible.
- A vegetarian diet would help to calm the malevolent Sun in the horoscope.
- Another effective remedy is to feed an ox, which is revered in Hindu mythology and religion.

- One should respect their father (or father figure) and seek their blessings, as it is considered as one of the most potent remedies.
- Individuals with an inauspicious Sun in their birth charts, should not accept gifts or accept anything for free. In this case, parents may be an exception.

We strongly advise consulting an experienced and expert Vedic astrologer for professional assessment of your horoscope and further guidance. Please watch YouTube videos for correct pronuciation of the Chalisa, mantras, chants etc.

# CHAPTER 8

# Ādityahṛdayam

*Valmiki's Ramayana's Yudh Kanda* (6.105) is a Hindu devotional hymn dedicated to *Surya Dev*. Before fighting the demon king *Ravana*, sage *Agastya* recited this hymn to Lord *Rama* on the battlefield in Lanka. In this, the sage *Agastya* teaches *Shri Ram* how to worship *Surya Dev*.

*Tato yuddhapariśrāntaṃ samare cintayā sthitam .*
*rāvaṇaṃ cāgrato dṛṣṭvā yuddhāya samupasthitam || 1 ||*

*Daivataiśca samāgamya draṣṭumabhyāgato raṇam .*
*upāgamyābravīdrāmamagastyo bhagavān ṛṣiḥ || 2 ||*

*Rāma rāma mahābāho śṛṇu guhyaṃ sanātanam .*
*yena sarvānarīn vatsa samare vijayiṣyase || 3 ||*

*ādityahṛdayaṃ puṇyaṃ sarvaśatruvināśanam .*
*jayāvahaṃ japam nityam akṣayaṃ paramaṃ śivam || 4 ||*

We strongly advise consulting an experienced and expert Vedic astrologer for professional assessment of your horoscope and further guidance. Please watch YouTube videos for correct pronuciation of the Chalisa, mantras, chants etc.

*sarvamaṅgalamāṅgalyaṃ sarvapāpapraṇāśanam .*
*cintāśokapraśamanam āyurvardhanamuttamam || 5 ||*

*raśmimantaṃ samudyantaṃ devāsuranamaskṛtam .*
*pūjayasva vivasvantaṃ bhāskaraṃ bhuvaneśvaram || 6 ||*

*sarvadevātmako hyeṣa tejasvī raśmibhāvanaḥ .*
*eṣa devāsuragaṇāllm̐lokān pāti gabhastibhiḥ || 7 ||*

*eṣa brahmā ca viṣṇuśca śivaḥ skandaḥ prajāpatiḥ .*
*mahendro dhanadaḥ kālo yamaḥ somo hyapāṃ patiḥ || 8 ||*

*pitaro vasavaḥ sādhyā aśvinau maruto manuḥ .*
*vāyurvahniḥ prajāh prāṇa ṛtukartā prabhākaraḥ || 9 ||*

*ādityaḥ savitā sūryaḥ khagaḥ pūṣā gabhastimān .*
*suvarṇasadṛśo bhānurhiraṇyaretā divākaraḥ || 10 ||*

*haridaśvaḥ sahasrārciḥ saptasaptirmarīcimān .*
*timironmathanaḥ śambhustvaṣṭā mārtāṇḍakoṃ'śumān || 11 ||*

*hiraṇyagarbhaḥ śiśirastapano bhāskaro raviḥ .*
*agnigarbho'diteḥ putraḥ śaṅkhaḥ śiśiranāśanaḥ || 12 ||*

*vyomanāthastamobhedī ṛgyajuḥsāmapāragaḥ .*
*ghanavṛṣṭirapāṃ mitro vindhyavīthīplavaṅgamaḥ || 13 ||*

*ātapī maṇḍalī mṛtyuḥ piṅgalaḥ sarvatāpanaḥ .*
*kavirviśvo mahātejā raktaḥ sarvabhavodbhavaḥ || 14 ||*

*nakṣatragrahatārāṇāmadhipo viśvabhāvanaḥ .*
*tejasāmapi tejasvī dvādaśātmannamo'stu te || 15 ||*

*namaḥ pūrvāya giraye paścimāyādraye namaḥ .*
*jyotirgaṇānāṃ pataye dinādhipataye namaḥ || 16 ||*

*jayāya jayabhadrāya haryaśvāya namo namaḥ .*
*namo namaḥ sahasrāṃśo ādityāya namo namaḥ || 17 ||*

*nama ugrāya vīrāya sāraṅgāya namo namaḥ .*
*namaḥ padmaprabodhāya mārtāṇḍāya namo namaḥ || 18 ||*

*brahmeśānācyuteśāya sūryāyādityavarcase .*
*bhāsvate sarvabhakṣāya raudrāya vapuṣe namaḥ || 19 ||*

*tamoghnāya himaghnāya śatrughnāyāmitātmane .*
*kṛtaghnaghnāya devāya jyotiṣāṃ pataye namaḥ || 20 ||*

*taptacāmīkarābhāya vahnaye viśvakarmaṇe .*
*namastamo'bhinighnāya rucaye lokasākṣiṇe || 21 ||*

*nāśayatyeṣa vai bhūtaṃ tadeva sṛjati prabhuḥ .*
*pāyatyeṣa tapatyeṣa varṣatyeṣa gabhastibhiḥ || 22 ||*

*eṣa supteṣu jāgarti bhūteṣu pariniṣṭhitaḥ .*
*eṣa evāgnihotraṃ ca phalaṃ caivāgnihotriṇām || 23 ||*

*vedāśca kṛtavaścaiva kṛtūnāṃ phalameva ca .*
*yāni kṛtyāni lokeṣu sarva eṣa raviḥ prabhuḥ || 24 ||*

## || *Phalaśrutiḥ* ||

*enamāpatsu kṛcchreṣu kāntāreṣu bhayeṣu ca .*
*kīrtayan puruṣaḥ kaścinnāvasīdati rāghava || 25 ||*

*pūjayasvainamekāgro devadevaṃ jagatpatim .*
*etat triguṇitaṃ japtvā yuddheṣu vijayiṣyasi || 26 ||*

*asmin kṣaṇe mahābāho rāvaṇaṃ tvaṃ jahiṣyasi .*
*evamuktvā tadāgastyo jagāma sa yathāgatam || 27 ||*

*etacchrutvā mahātejā naṣṭaśoko'bhavattadā .*
*dhārayāmāsa suprīto rāghavaḥ prayatātmavān || 28 ||*

*ādityaṃ prekṣya japtvedaṃ paraṃ harṣamavāptavān .*
*trirācamya śucirbhūtvā dhanurādāya vīryavān || 29 ||*

*rāvaṇaṃ prekṣya hṛṣṭātmā yuddhāya samupāgamat .*
*sarvayatnena mahatā vadhe tasya dhṛto'bhavat || 30 ||*

*atha raviravadannirīkṣya rāmaṃ*
*muditamanāḥ paramaṃ prahṛṣyamāṇaḥ .*
*niśicarapatisaṃkṣayaṃ viditvā*
*suragaṇamadhyagato vacastvareti || 31 ||*

|| *iti ādityahṛdayam* ||

We strongly advise consulting an experienced and expert Vedic astrologer for professional assessment of your horoscope and further guidance. Please watch YouTube videos for correct pronuciation of the Chalisa, mantras, chants etc.

CHAPTER 9

# Twenty-one Names of Shri Surya Dev

Reciting these twenty-one names every morning and night, just once, is supposed to cleanse the body of all disease, remove obstacles to wealth and happiness in one's life, and remove negative *karma*.

***Eka Vimshati Namavali***: These are the 21 names of *Surya Dev* with **meaning:**

1 विकर्तन
**Transliteration:** Vikartana
**Meaning:** *The one who destroys all dangers*

2 विवस्वान
**Transliteration:** Vivaswana
**Meaning:** Luminescent

We strongly advise consulting an experienced and expert Vedic astrologer for professional assessment of your horoscope and further guidance. Please watch YouTube videos for correct pronuciation of the Chalisa, mantras, chants etc.

3 मार्तण्ड

**Transliteration:** Martanda

**Meaning:** The one who has emerged from the golden egg

4 भास्कर

**Transliteration:** Bhaskara

**Meaning:** The enlightening one

5 रवि

**Transliteration:** Ravi

**Meaning:** The one who roars

6 लोकप्रकाशक

**Transliteration:** Lokaprakashaka

**Meaning:** The illuminator of the worlds

7 श्रीमान

**Transliteration:** Shrimana

**Meaning:** One who possesses the knowledge of Yoga, Gentleman

8 लोक चक्षु

**Transliteration:** Loka Chakshu

**Meaning:** Eye of the world

9 ग्रहेश्वर

**Transliteration:** Graheshwara

**Meaning:** The lord of all the planets

We strongly advise consulting an experienced and expert Vedic astrologer for professional assessment of your horoscope and further guidance. Please watch YouTube videos for correct pronuciation of the Chalisa, mantras, chants etc.

10 लोक साक्षी
**Transliteration:** Loka Sakshi
**Meaning:** Witness of the world

11 त्रिलोकेश
**Transliteration:** Trilokesha
**Meaning:** The lord of the three worlds

12 कर्ता
**Transliteration:** Karta
**Meaning:** The executor

13 हर्ता
**Transliteration:** Harta
**Meaning:** The destroyer

14 तमिस्रहा
**Transliteration:** Tamisraha
**Meaning:** The remover of darkness

15 तपन
**Transliteration:** Tapana
**Meaning:** The one who heats up

16 तापन
**Transliteration:** Tapana
**Meaning:** The one who burns

We strongly advise consulting an experienced and expert Vedic astrologer for professional assessment of your horoscope and further guidance. Please watch YouTube videos for correct pronuciation of the Chalisa, mantras, chants etc.

17 शुचि
**Transliteration:** Shuchi
**Meaning:** The one who is pure

18 सप्ताश्ववाहन
**Transliteration:** Saptashvavahana
**Meaning:** Whose chariot is drawn by seven horses

19 गभस्तिहस्त
**Transliteration:** Gabhastihasta
**Meaning:** Whose hands are rays alike

20 ब्रईखा
**Transliteration:** Brahma
**Meaning:** The creator of the world

21 सर्वदेवनमस्कृत
**Transliteration:** Sarvadevanamaskrita
**Meaning:** Worshipped by all the gods

।। इति श्री सूर्य एकविंशतिनामावलिः सम्पूण ।।

We strongly advise consulting an experienced and expert Vedic astrologer for professional assessment of your horoscope and further guidance. Please watch YouTube videos for correct pronuciation of the Chalisa, mantras, chants etc.

# CHAPTER 10

# Surya Ashtottara Shatanamavali Stotra

## 108 names of Surya Dev

### Surya Ashtottara Shatanamavali Stotra

108 names of *Surya Dev* are known as Ashtottara *Shatanamavali of Surya. Ashtottara Shatanam*, translates to "hundred and eight names" (*nama*). The names of the Sun given below are from ancient manuscripts that detail all of the Sun's representations. This includes the Trinity, the *Yugas*, the other planets, the king *Indra*, and even the *Manu* of the current universe.

Reciting the names listed below not only strengthens the Sun in your horoscope but also brings tremendous focus into your life. It is also believed that reciting these ancient Sun names while standing facing the Sun burns our *Sanchita Karma* and unfulfilled desires quickly. The best time to recite is during the Sun's *hora* or at sunrise.

We strongly advise consulting an experienced and expert Vedic astrologer for professional assessment of your horoscope and further guidance. Please watch YouTube videos for correct pronuciation of the Chalisa, mantras, chants etc.

The *Ashtottara Shatanamavali Stotra* is a hymn in which one hundred of the Lord's names are recounted. Composing hymns with names for the main deity of worship likely became popular amongst the various sects of Vedic tradition (*Shaivism, Shaktism,* and *Vaishnavism*) as they expanded and spread throughout the world.

1. ॐ अरुणाय नमः। *Aruna*: means the one colored Reddish Brown
2. ॐ शरण्याय नमः। *Sharanya*: The One Who Provides Sanctuary
3. ॐ करुणारससिन्धवे नमः। *Karunarasa sindhu*: The Ocean of the Feeling of Empathy
4. ॐ असमानबलाय नमः। *Asmanabala*: The One with Unparalleled Strength.
5. ॐ आर्तरक्षकाय नमः। *Arta-rakshaka*: The Protector from Misery
6. ॐ आदित्याय नमः। *Aditya*: The son of *Aditi*
7. ॐ आदिभूताय नमः। *Adibhuta*: the first of the beings
8. ॐ अखिलागमवेदिने नमः। *Akhila-gamavedin*: The Knower of All Scriptures
9. ॐ अच्युताय नमः। *Achyuta*: The Imperishable
10. ॐ अखिलज्ञाय नमः। *Akhilagya*: The Apprehender of Everything
11. ॐ अनन्ताय नमः। *Ananta*: The Unbounded One
12. ॐ इनाय नमः। *Ina*: The Strong One
13. ॐ विश्वरूपाय नमः। *Vishvarupa*: The One with an All-Pervading Form
14. ॐ इज्याय नमः। *Ijya*: The One to be Revered
15. ॐ इन्द्राय नमः। *Indra*: Leader of the Gods

We strongly advise consulting an experienced and expert Vedic astrologer for professional assessment of your horoscope and further guidance. Please watch YouTube videos for correct pronuciation of the Chalisa, mantras, chants etc.

16. ॐ भानवे नमः । *Bhanu*: The Bright One
17. ॐ इन्दिरामन्दिराप्ताय नमः । *Indriramandirapta*: The One Who Has Gained the Abode of Indira (Lakshmi)
18. ॐ वन्दनीयाय नमः ।, *Vandaniya*: The Praiseworthy One
19. ॐ ईशाय नमः ।, *Isha*: The Lord
20. ॐ सुप्रसन्नाय नमः ।, *Suprasanna*: The Very Bright One
21. ॐ सुशीलाय नमः ।, *Sushila*: The Good-Natured One
22. ॐ सुवर्चसे नमः ।, *Suvarchas*: The Brilliant One
23. ॐ वसुप्रदाय नमः ।, *Vasuprada*: The Bestower of wealth
24. ॐ वसवे नमः ।, *Vasu*: The Deva (The Excellent One)
25. ॐ वासुदेवाय नमः ।, *Vasudeva*: Shri Krishna
26. ॐ उज्ज्वल नमः ।, *Ujjaval*: The Blazing One
27. ॐ उग्ररूपाय नमः ।, *Ugrarupa*: The One with a Ferce Form
28. ॐ ऊर्ध्वगाय नमः ।, *Urdhvaga*: The One Who Rises Up
29. ॐ विवस्वते नमः ।, *Vivasvat*: The One Who Shines Forth
30. ॐ उद्यत्किरणजालाय नमः ।, *Udhatkiranajala*: The One Who Produces a Lattice of Rising Beams of Light
31. ॐ हृषीकेशाय नमः ।, *Hrishikesha*: Lord of the Senses
32. ॐ ऊर्जस्वलाय नमः ।, *Urjasvala*: The Mighty One
33. ॐ वीराय नमः ।, *Vira*: The Brave One
34. ॐ निर्जराय नमः ।, *Nirjara*: The Imperishable One
35. ॐ जयाय नमः ।, *Jaya*: The Victorious One
36. ॐ ऊरुद्वयाभावरूपयुक्तसारथये नमः ।, *Urudvaya-bhavaroo-payukta-sarathi*: The One Whose Charioteer has a Form without a Pair of Thighs
37. ॐ ऋषिवन्द्याय नमः ।, *Rishivandya*: The One Worshipped by Rishis
38. ॐ रुग्घन्त्रे नमः ।, *Rugghantr*: The Destroyer of Disease
39. ॐ ऋक्षचक्रचराय नमः ।, *Rikshachakrachara*: The One Who Moves Through the Wheel of Stars

We strongly advise consulting an experienced and expert Vedic astrologer for professional assessment of your horoscope and further guidance. Please watch YouTube videos for correct pronuciation of the Chalisa, mantras, chants etc.

40. ॐ ऋजुस्वभावचित्ताय नमः ।, *Rijusva-bhavachitta*: The One Whose Mind by Nature is Sincere
41. ॐ नित्यस्तुत्याय नमः ।, *Nityastutya*: The One Who is Fit to Praised Always
42. ॐ ऋकारमातृकावर्णरूपाय नमः ।, *Rikaramatrikavarna-rupa*: The One Who has the Form of the Letter *Rikara*
43. ॐ उज्ज्वलतेजसे नमः ।, *Ujjvalateja*s: The One with a Blazing Brilliance
44. ॐ ऋक्षाधिनाथमित्राय नमः ।, *Rikshadhinathamitra*: The Friend of the Lord of Stars (the Moon)
45. ॐ पुष्कराक्षाय नमः ।, *Pushkaraksha*: The Lotus-Eyed One
46. ॐ लुप्तदन्ताय नमः ।, *Luptadanta*: The One Whose Teeth are Lost
47. ॐ शान्ताय नमः ।, *Shanta*: Pacified, Calm
48. ॐ कान्तिदाय नमः ।, *Kantida*: The Bestower of Beauty
49. ॐ घनाय नमः ।, *Ghana*: The Destroyer
50. ॐ कनत्कनकभूषाय नमः ।, *Kanatkanaka-bhusha*: The Brilliant Golden Ornament
51. ॐ खद्योताय नमः ।, *Khadyota*: The Light of the Sky
52. ॐ लूनिताखिलदैत्याय नमः ।, *Lunitakhila-daitya*: The Destroyer of All Demons
53. ॐ सत्यानन्दस्वरूपिणे नमः ।, *Satyananda-svarupin*: The One Whose Nature is True Bliss
54. ॐ अपवर्गप्रदाय नमः ।, *Apavarga-prada*: The Bestower of Liberation
55. ॐ आर्तशरण्याय नमः ।, *Arta-sharanya*: The Provider of Shelter to the Distressed
56. ॐ एकाकिने नमः ।, *Ekakin*: The solitary One
57. ॐ भगवते नमः ।, *Bhagavat*: The Divine One

We strongly advise consulting an experienced and expert Vedic astrologer for professional assessment of your horoscope and further guidance. Please watch YouTube videos for correct pronuciation of the Chalisa, mantras, chants etc.

58. ॐ सृष्टिस्थित्यन्तकारिणे नमः ।, *Srishti-sthityantakarin*: The One Who Makes the Creation, Maintenance, and End
59. ॐ गुणात्मने नमः ।, *Gunatman*: The One with Qualities
60. ॐ घृणिभृते नमः ।, *Ghrinibhrit*: The One Who Possesses Light
61. ॐ बृहते नमः ।, *Brihat*: The Great One
62. ॐ ब्रईखणे नमः ।, *Brahman*: The Eternal Brahman
63. ॐ ऐश्वर्यदाय नमः ।, *Eshvaryada*: The Bestower of Power
64. ॐ शर्वाय नमः ।, *Sharva*: The One that Injures
65. ॐ हरिदश्वाय नमः ।, *Haridashva*: The One with Tawny Horses
66. ॐ शौरये नमः ।, *Shauri*: The Heroic One
67. ॐ दशदिक्संप्रकाशाय नमः ।, *Dashadiksam-prakasha*: The One Who Shines in Ten Directions
68. ॐ भक्तवश्याय नमः ।, *Bhakta-vashya*: The One Who is Attentive to the Devotees
69. ॐ ओजस्कराय नमः ।, *Ojaskara*: The Maker of Power
70. ॐ जयिने नमः ।, *Jayin*: The victorious One
71. ॐ जगदानन्दहेतवे नमः ।, *Jagadanandahetu*: The Cause of Joy for the World
72. ॐ जन्ममृत्युजराव्याधिवर्जिताय नमः ।, *Janma-mrityu-jara-vyadhi-varjita*: The One Who is Free from Birth, Death, Old Age, Suffering, etc.
73. ॐ उच्चस्थान समारूढरथस्थाय नमः ।, *Uchchasthana sama-rudha-rathastha*: The One Established in a Chariot that Moves with Lofty Steps
74. ॐ असुरारये नमः ।, *Asurari*: The Enemy of the Demons
75. ॐ कमनीयकराय नमः ।, *Kamaniyakara*: The Fulfiller of Desires

We strongly advise consulting an experienced and expert Vedic astrologer for professional assessment of your horoscope and further guidance. Please watch YouTube videos for correct pronuciation of the Chalisa, mantras, chants etc.

76. ॐ अब्जवल्लभाय नमः ।, *Abjavallabha*: The Most Beloved of *Abja (Dhanvantari)*
77. ॐ अन्तर्बहिः प्रकाशाय नमः ।, *Antarbahih prakasha*: The One with Inner and Outer Brilliance
78. ॐ अचिन्त्याय नमः ।, *Achintya*: The Inconceivable One
79. ॐ आत्मरूपिणे नमः ।, *Atmarupin*: The Form of Atman
80. ॐ अच्युताय नमः ।, *Achyuta*: The Imperishable One
81. ॐ अमरेशाय नमः ।, *Amaresha*: The Lord of Immortals
82. ॐ परस्मै ज्योतिषे नमः ।, *Para Jyotish*: The Supreme Light
83. ॐ अहस्कराय नमः ।, *Ahaskara*: The Maker of the Day
84. ॐ रवये नमः ।, *Ravi*: The One Who Roars
85. ॐ हरये नमः ।, *Hari*: The Remover (of Sin)
86. ॐ परमात्मने नमः ।, *Paramatman*: The Supreme Being
87. ॐ तरुणाय नमः ।, *Taruna*: The Youthful One
88. ॐ वरेण्याय नमः ।, *Varenya*: The Most Excellent One
89. ॐ ग्रहाणांपतये नमः ।, *Grahanam Pati*: The Lord of Planets
90. ॐ भास्कराय नमः ।, *Bhaskara*: The Maker of Light
91. ॐ आदिमध्यान्तरहिताय नमः ।, *Adimadhyantarahita*: The One Who is Solitary in the Beginning, Middle, and End
92. ॐ सौख्यप्रदाय नमः ।, *Saukhyaprada*: The Bestower of Happiness
93. ॐ सकलजगतांपतये नमः ।, *Sakalajagatam Pati*: The Lord of All Worlds
94. ॐ सूर्याय नमः ।, *Surya*: The Powerful One, or The Brilliant One
95. ॐ कवये नमः ।, *Kavi*: The Wise One
96. ॐ नारायणाय नमः ।, *Narayana*: The One Whom Men Approach
97. ॐ परेशाय नमः ।, *Paresha*: The Highest Lord

We strongly advise consulting an experienced and expert Vedic astrologer for professional assessment of your horoscope and further guidance. Please watch YouTube videos for correct pronuciation of the Chalisa, mantras, chants etc.

98. ॐ तेजोरूपाय नमः।, *Tejorupa*: The One with the Form of Fire
99. ॐ हिरण्यगर्भाय नमः।, *Hiranyagarbha*: The Golden Source (of the Universe)
100. ॐ सम्पत्कराय नमः।, *Sampatkara*: The Maker of Success
101. ॐ ऐं इष्टार्थदाय नमः।, *Aem Istarthada*: The Bestower of the Desired Object
102. ॐ अं सुप्रसन्नाय नमः।, *Am Suprasanna*: The Very Bright One
103. ॐ श्रीमते नमः।, *Shrimat*: The Glorious One
104. ॐ श्रेयसे नमः।, *Shreyas*: The Most Excellent One
105. ॐ सौख्यदायिने नमः।, *Saukhyadayin*: The Bestower of Enjoyments
106. ॐ दीप्तमूर्तये नमः।, *Diptamurti:* The One with a Blazing Form
107. ॐ निखिलागमवेद्याय नमः।, *Nikhilagamavedya:* The Knower of All Scriptures
108. ॐ नित्यानन्दाय नमः। *Nityananda*: The One Who is Always Blissful

# Conclusion and Prayers

The Sun is of utmost significance in astrology; hence, it's crucial to critically study the Sun's position when analyzing a birth chart. The Sun is the soul of our solar system and the source of light and life on Earth. Engaging in worship or remedy is beneficial regardless of where the Sun sits in your natal chart and whether it is auspicious, malefic, or neutral.

The problems you face will generally get better if you practice the remedies and incorporate them into your daily activities. This is because the Sun, the source of light for everyone, including all other planets, will lessen the adverse effects and usher in peace, love, health, and happiness in your life.

We strongly advise consulting an experienced and expert Vedic astrologer for professional assessment of your horoscope and further guidance. Please watch YouTube videos for correct pronuciation of the Chalisa, mantras, chants etc.

Kindly accept my prayers for you are your family:

ॐ असतो मा सद्गमय ।
तमसो मा ज्योतिर्गमय ।
मृत्योर्मा अमृतं गमय ।
ॐ शान्तिः शान्तिः शान्तिः ।।

***asato ma sadgamaya***
***tamaso ma jyotirgamaya***
***mrtyorma amrtam gamaya***
***om shanti shanti shanti.***

Lead me from the unreality to the truth.
Lead me from darkness to light.
Lead me from death to immortality
Om Peace Peace Peace.

सर्वेषां स्वस्तिर्भवतु ।
सर्वेषां शान्तिर्भवतु ।
सर्वेषां पूर्नं भवतु ।
सर्वेषां मङ्गलं भवतु ।।

***Sarveśām Svastir Bhavatu***
***Sarveśām Shāntir Bhavatu***
***Sarveśām Pūrnam Bhavatu***
***Sarveśām Maṇgalam Bhavatu***

May there be happiness in all
May there be peace in all
May there be completeness in all
May there be success in all

We strongly advise consulting an experienced and expert Vedic astrologer for professional assessment of your horoscope and further guidance. Please watch YouTube videos for correct pronuciation of the Chalisa, mantras, chants etc.

ॐ द्यौः शान्तिरन्तरिक्षं शान्तिः
पृथिवी शान्तिरापः शान्तिरोषधयः शान्तिः ।
वनस्पतयः शान्तिर्विश्वेदेवाः शान्तिर्ब्रह्म शान्तिः
सर्वं शान्तिः शान्तिरेव शान्तिः सा मा शान्तिरेधि ।।
ॐ शान्तिः शान्तिः शान्तिः ।।

***om dhyauh shantir***
***antariksham shantih***
***prithví shantir***
***apah shantir***
***oshadhayah shantih***
***vanaspatayah shantir***
***vishve devah shantih***
***bramah shantih***
***sarvam shantih***
***shantir eva shantih***
***sa ma shantir-edhi***

OM Peace be in the universe,
May there be peace be in the atmosphere,
May there be peace be on earth,
May there be peace be in the waters,
May there be peace be in the herbs,
May there be peace be in the vegetation,
May there be peace be in the elements,
May there be Peace of the Supreme,
May there be peace be everywhere,
May there be peace, only peace,
May there be peace in my mind and heart.

We strongly advise consulting an experienced and expert Vedic astrologer for professional assessment of your horoscope and further guidance. Please watch YouTube videos for correct pronuciation of the Chalisa, mantras, chants etc.

ॐ सर्वे भवन्तु सुखिनः
सर्वे सन्तु निरामयाः ।
सर्वे भद्राणि पश्यन्तु
मा कश्चिद्दुःखभाग्भवेत् ।
ॐ शान्तिः शान्तिः शान्तिः ।।

***Om Sarve Bhavantu Sukhinah***
***Sarve Santu Niraamayaah***
***Sarve Bhadraanni Pashyantu***
***Maa Kashcid-Duhkha-Bhaag-Bhavet***
***Om Shaantih Shaantih Shaantih***

O' thee merciful Lord, bless all with happiness,
free all from illness and misery,
please bestow Thy divine blessing such that
all may realize eternal Bliss.
Om, Peace, Peace, Peace

We strongly advise consulting an experienced and expert Vedic astrologer for professional assessment of your horoscope and further guidance. Please watch YouTube videos for correct pronuciation of the Chalisa, mantras, chants etc.

# Appendix

## THE SEVEN HORSES OF SURYA DEV (SUN GOD)

It is customary to praise the Sun god with the mantra ***'saptāśva rathamārūḍham pracaṁḍam kaśyapātmajam śvēta padmadharam dēvam tam sūryam praṇamāmyaham'*. The** *mantra* **means** 'my salutations to the Sun God, who rides on a chariot with seven horses, the brightest of lights, son of Sage Kashyapa, and who holds the white lotus flower' (*Sūryāṣṭakam* 2nd *mantra*).

The *Sanātana dharma* considers *Sun* as a form of the Vedas, the *Ṛgyajussāmapāragaḥ (Āditya Hṛudayam, 13th mantra)*. The seven horses dragging the chariot are the *Vedic* meters (*chandas*) viz., *Gāyatrī, Triṣtup, Anuṣtup, Jagatī, Uṣnik, Paṅkti* and *Bṛhati* as revealed in the *Veda Saṃhitas* and later in *Vhiṣṇu* and *Sūrya Purāṇas*. While the reins of the chariot are held by a charioteer named *Aruḍa* (one who is devoid of thighs). At the same time, according to the *Purāṇas*, the names of the seven horses of the Sun are *Jaya, Vijaya, Ajaya, Jitaprāṇa, Jitaśrama, Manōjava* and *Jitakrodha* (source: *Bhaviṣya Purāṇa*). These names refer to different phases of light transmission by the Sun throughout the day, which are the pinnacle of power.

The seven horses represent amongst other things: the seven chakras in our spine, the rainbow's seven colors, and the seven days of the week. These chakras and the meridians that run through them are the repository for our '*Sanchita*' karma. It is the cause of our death, rebirth, and death cycle. Similarly, the Sun controls the chariot of our lives by firmly holding onto the reins connected to our seven chakras and directing the flow of our lives from birth to death, just as *Aruna*, the charioteer of the Sun God's chariot, controls the reins of the seven horses and directs them from the east to the west in our sky. The basic seven elements that represent the human body are the skin, blood, flesh, fat, bone, marrow and semen, and this body chariots these elements. *Āditya Paramātma* is the in the form of consciousness that manages these elements (*Garuḍa Purāṇa* 15 (27, 62); *Śārṅgadhara Saṃhita* 1-5-12). The Surya Dev is in the form of *Arka* in *kunḍalinī* (snake shape) that stretches from *Mūlādhāra* to *Sahasrāra* and the seven horses form the seven *chakrasthanas* in the path (source: *Devī Bhāgavata Purāṇa*).

It is believed that reciting the names of the seven horses can activate the seven chakras.

We strongly advise consulting an experienced and expert Vedic astrologer for professional assessment of your horoscope and further guidance. Please watch YouTube videos for correct pronuciation of the Chalisa, mantras, chants etc.

## HORA (HOUR) OF SURYA (SUN) ACCORDING TO VEDIC ASTROLOGY

Each day, the hour (*hora*) of the Sun is the best time to meditate. Perform Sun salutations, and chant Sun (*Surya*) mantras during these times if possible. The Sun's Hora is favorable for all political work, dealing with and meeting politicians, leaders, and government officials applying for jobs, dealing with the courts, buying and selling, and taking risks.

An hour of the day, known as a hora, is controlled by a specific planet. The horas are either beneficial or destructive for pursuits, according to the ruling planet. As a result, twenty-four horas for each of the seven days of the week are controlled by the *navagrahas*, or the seven astrological planets. Depending on the prevailing planet, the horas can either help or damage certain endeavors. This information can be used to determine when it would be best to launch a new project.

For example, if you'd like to check the hora on Wednesday at 10 a.m. Your local newspaper or smartphone lists the sunrise time as 6.30 a.m. and the sunset time as 6:00 p.m. Divide 11.5 hours by 12, and each planet controls 57 minutes 30 seconds (approximately 1 hour)—similarly, planets in the order of 62 minutes 30 seconds each control 12.5 hours of the night. The hour given below is an approximation based on the assumption that sunrise occurs ideally at 6 a.m. and sunset occurs ideally at 6 p.m.

| Day | Time |
|---|---|
| Sunday | 7AM, 2PM, 9PM |
| Monday | 11AM, 6PM |
| Tuesday | 8AM, 3PM, 10PM |
| Wednesday | Midday, 7PM |
| Thursday | 9AM, 4PM, 11PM |
| Friday | 1PM, 8PM |
| Saturday | 10AM, 5PM, Midnight |

We strongly advise consulting an experienced and expert Vedic astrologer for professional assessment of your horoscope and further guidance. Please watch YouTube videos for correct pronuciation of the Chalisa, mantras, chants etc.

# AS PER THE HINDU CALENDAR, SUN GOD IS WORSHIPPED AS FOLLOWS

| Name of the Month as per Vedic Science | Equivalent Western period of the year | How is Surya Dev referred to, in this month? | Meaning of the name |
|---|---|---|---|
| *Pausha* | Jan – Feb | *Bhaga* | One who gives livelihood |
| *Magha* | Feb – Mar | *Twashtha* | Remover of obstacles |
| *Phalguna* | Mar – Apr | *Vishnu* | Shri Maha-Vishnu, the protector |
| *Chaitra* | Apr – May | *Dhata* | Benevolent donor |
| *Vaisaka* | May – Jun | *Aryamaa* | Noble minded |
| *Jyeshta* | Jun – Jul | *Mitra* | Friend |
| *Aashada* | Jul – Aug | *Varuna* | Rain God |
| *Shraavana* | Aug – Sep | *Indra* | King of Devas |
| *Bhadra* | Sep – Oct | *Vivasvan* | Endowed with bright rays |
| *Ashvin* | Oct – Nov | *Puusa* | Nourisher |
| *Kartik* | Nov – Dec | *Parjanya* | Benevolent donor |
| *Agahana* | Dec – Jan | *Anshu* | Sun rays |

## SUN WORSHIP IN ANCIENT CULTURES ALL OVER THE WORLD

The sun is the source of wisdom since light is nearly universally associated with enlightenment or illumination and gives light and life to the entire cosmos. Humans have always relied on the Sun for light, warmth, and food, despite numerous technological advances that have given us more independence. Solar energy's significance in reducing our carbon footprint reminds us that we still rely on Sun for our survival.

Evidence shows that the Neolithic people saw the winter solstice as a representation of life's inevitable triumph. The megalithic buildings built by Neolithic peoples, such as Stonehenge in England (built in 3000 BCE) and Newgrange in Ireland (3200 BCE), are proof of the significance of the Sun in their worldviews, even though we may never fully comprehend the religious beliefs of these peoples. The design of Newgrange allows a shaft of sunshine to shine into the passage's entrance on the days preceding and following the winter solstice.

Two millennia before the Common Era began, a Sun God cult worshipped in anthropomorphic form was discovered on the slate cliffs of Kazakhstan. No written records describe this religion or the worship it included, but several engravings, particularly at the *Tamgaly* cultic site, depict a humanized "Sun," occasionally accompanied by a zoomorphic figure. Processions were probably made to these cultic sites, and these beliefs were tied to the cyclical nature of the seasons.

We strongly advise consulting an experienced and expert Vedic astrologer for professional assessment of your horoscope and further guidance. Please watch YouTube videos for correct pronuciation of the Chalisa, mantras, chants etc.

Sun worship has been practiced by many cultures and religions throughout history, and sun deities have frequently served as the focal point of those religions. The Nabateans, who constructed the city of Petra in Jordan, the Incas in Peru, Shintoism in Japan, and other cultures and religions have all historically practiced substantial Sun worship. The sun's influence on religious belief can also be found in Zoroastrianism, Mithraism, Roman religion, and among the Druids of England, Aztecs of Mexico, Incas of Peru, and many Native Americans.

The spirituality of the Nabateans was based on the Sun. ***Dushara***, one of their deities, was associated with the Sun and was worshiped from temple rooftops. Evidence suggests that Petra, a famous Nabatean city in Jordan that dates back to 400 BCE, had several monuments depicting the equinoxes and solstices. After Rome annexed Nabetea, the god face was still found on the local coinage. The Sun God ***Re*** was the most important deity in ancient Egypt and had held this status since the beginning of that civilization's existence.

***Inti***, the Sun God, was one of the most significant deities for the Inca civilization in Peru, South America. ***Quilla***, ***Inti's*** wife, was the Moon, goddess of women and female chores. The Inca, or emperor, was considered ***Inti's*** son. According to South American legend, the Inca ruler *Pachacuti* attained power over the land from a mirrored sun disk. The yearly *Inti Ramyi* festival celebrated in honor of Sun, which occurs during the summer solstice, is still considered a time for drinking, singing, and dancing. Most Inca architecture was planned and constructed to support Sun worship, with pillars placed to indicate the Sun's location at various solstices. According to the legend of *Manco Inca* and *Mama Ocllo*, they were sent by their father, the Sun, and were born on the sun's island within the sacred Lake Titicaca.

Sun worship was vital in the pre-Columbian civilizations of Mexico and Peru. The Sun played an important role in myth and ritual in Mexican and Peruvian ancient religions. The Sun gods ***Huitzilopochtli*** and ***Tezcatlipoca*** demanded human sacrifice in Aztec beliefs. The Sun Dance of the Plains Indians is a prime example of one of North America's most well-known Sun worshiping cults. In particular, the Sun Dance ceremony is a solemn vigil for achieving deeper awareness (power) during difficult times. This dance is viewed as a renewal of man's relationship with life, the earth, and the growing season. The Inca culture is thought to have settled in what is now Ecuador, Peru, Bolivia, a portion of Chile, and Argentina. With Spanish colonization and the imposed Catholic religion, the Inca empire's subjects were forced to stop worshiping Sun God ***Inti***.

During the Bronze Age, the Sumerian Sun God ***Utu*** (in Akkadian ***Šamaš***), also the god of justice, played an essential role in Mesopotamia and because the sun illuminated the entire sky, ***Utu*** oversaw everything that happened during the day. He was also thought to bring warmth and light to the land, and plants and crops could not grow without him. ***Utu*** was a member of an astral triad that included the lunar God ***Nanna*** (***Sin*** in Akkadian) and the Goddess of love and war, ***Inanna***, whose symbol was the morning star.

***Amaterasu***, the Sun Goddess, is the most significant deity in the Shinto religion and rules the High Celestial

Plain. One popular legend has ***Amaterasu*** locking herself in a cave after an argument with another God. According to the myth, the world was plunged into total darkness when ***Amaterasu*** vanished, and it wasn't until she emerged from the cave that the sun came out again. The Japanese emperors are thought to be *Amaterasu's* descendants, and the Japanese state is still represented by solar emblems.

In the myth of the Sun God's voyage across the heavenly ocean, the Sun begins its journey as the young God ***Kheper***, appears at noon in the zenith as the full-grown Sun, ***Ra***, and arrives in the evening as the old Sun God: ***Atum***. When Pharaoh *Ikhnaton* reformed Egyptian religion, he adopted the cult of the ancient deity ***Ra-Horakhte*** as ***Aton***, an older name for the Sun's disk. The Sun's qualities as creator and nourisher of the Earth and its inhabitants are extolled by ***Akhenaton***. The person solely responsible for bringing monotheism—the worship of one God—to ancient Egypt was Akhenaten.

Sun festivals were celebrated in medieval Iran as a pre-Islamic heritage. The Indo-European character of sun worship can also be seen in the depiction of the solar deity, drawn in his carriage, usually drawn by white horses, which is common to many Indo-European peoples and appears in Indo-Iranian, Greco-Roman, and Scandinavian mythology.

There were two sun gods in Greece: *Apollo* and *Helio*s. The Sun God, ***Helios***, resembled ***Ra*** in many ways, and was revered by the Greeks. Homer describes ***Helios*** as "giving light to both gods and men." ***Helios*** was conceived as a beautiful deity with a tremendous and powerful gold crown. Every day, he rode a chariot through the sky to the ocean, the perfect river that encircled the earth, ***Gaea***. Every year, the ***Helios*** cult celebrated with an impressive ritual that involved a massive chariot pulled by horses off the end of a cliff and into the sea. Homer describes ***Helios'*** chariot as being drawn by fire bulls, but Pindar describes them as "fire-throwing horses." According to Hesiod, ***Eos*** was a Greek solar Goddess associated with the *aurora borealis* and the daughter of the titans ***Hyperion*** and ***Tea***.

As part of the *Mithraic* cult, the ancient Persians celebrated the accent of the sun in the sky every day. Scholars have determined that honoring the sun was integral to the *Mithraism* ritual and ceremony. ***Heliodromus***, or sun carrier, was one of the highest ranks one could attain in a *Mithraic* temple. The Christian resurrection narrative may have its roots in the *Mithraic* tale.

Sun worship became more popular in later periods of Roman history, eventually leading to what has been dubbed "solar monotheism." Almost all the gods of the time possessed solar qualities, and both ***Christ*** and ***Mithra*** inherited the traits of solar deities. The feast of *Sol Invictus* (Unconquered Sun) on December 25 was widely celebrated, and this date was eventually adopted by Christians as Christmas, the birthday of ***Christ***. Later Sun worship was considered idolatrous—and thus forbidden—once Christianity gained a religious foothold, according to William Tyler Olcott in Sun Lore of All Ages, published in 1914.

Some other notable mentions are

**Name**: ***Sol***
**Religion**: Norse Gods and Goddesses
**Realms**: Sun goddess

**Name**: ***Arinna***
**Religion**: Hittite Mythology
**Realms**: Sun goddess

**Name**: ***Huitzilopochtli***
**Religion**: Aztec gods and goddesses
**Realms**: God associated with the Sun, also considered a war god

**Name**: ***Kinich Ahau***
**Religion**: Mayan mythology
**Realms**: Solar Deity

**Name**: ***Shamash***
**Religion**: Ancient Mesopotamian
**Realms**: Sun God for the people living in the region between Tigris and Euphrates.

**Name**: ***Lugh***
**Religion**: Celtic religion of ancient Europe
**Realms**: God linked with the Sun and light

**Name**: ***Maui***
**Religion**: Polynesian
**Realms**: God associated with the Sun, and a hero

**Name**: ***Yhi***
**Religion**: Australian Aboriginal God
**Realms**: Goddess of light, creation, and the Sun

We strongly advise consulting an experienced and expert Vedic astrologer for professional assessment of your horoscope and further guidance. Please watch YouTube videos for correct pronuciation of the Chalisa, mantras, chants etc.

## STEP-BY-STEP GUIDE TO PREFORM SURYA NAMASKAR

If you only have 10 minutes to practice, go through this ancient series of yoga postures known as Sun Salutations. This posture sequence dates back over 2,500 years to when Vedic cultures in India revered the sun. Salutations were thought to be a literal salute to the sunrise and to prepare the body for everything that would happen during the day. This posture sequence is a series of motions that begin and end with *Tadasana* (Mountain Pose). The poses take you through various stretches, forward folds, and backbends that generate heat and occur in a rhythmic cadence that corresponds to your breath. Your transition from one posture to the next is signaled by the beginning of inhalation, and then followed by a pause in the breath, and then executing the yoga pose a. Your next transition is signaled by the beginning of an exhale. The sequence's trajectory is predictable and cyclical, making it easy to become quietly absorbed in the looping repeated motions.

We strongly advise consulting an experienced and expert Vedic astrologer for professional assessment of your horoscope and further guidance. Please watch YouTube videos for correct pronuciation of the Chalisa, mantras, chants etc.

**Tadasana** (Mountain Pose)

Place your feet together and your arms by your sides. In *Tadasana*, distribute your weight evenly between your feet and turn your palms forward. Allow yourself to take a slow, steady breath. In *Anjali Mudra*, bring your palms together at the center of your chest to find your own center (also known as Salutation Seal or, quite simply, prayer hands).

**Hastasana** (Urdhva Hastasana)

In *Urdhva Hastasana*, inhale and sweep your arms straight to the sides and up alongside your ears. Your palms should face each other; you can bring them together if you want. Bring your heart and arms up to the sun. You can also take a slight backend, lifting your chest and leaning your upper body slightly, if you prefer.

**Uttanasana** (Standing Forward Bend)

Exhale and bring your chest to your thighs by bending forward at the hips. Draw your knees toward your hips to keep your legs strong. Relax your shoulders and neck. In *Uttanasana*, your hands can rest on your shins, ankles, or blocks.

**Ardha Uttanasana** (Half Standing Forward Bend)

In *Ardha Uttanasana*, inhale as you lift your chest parallel to the mat. (As the pose's name suggests, you'll be halfway to standing.) Pull your shoulder blades away from your ears and lengthen your spine. You can either leave your palms or fingertips on the floor or bring them up to your shins or blocks.

**Plank Position**

Exhale and return to Plank Pose, similar to the top of a push-up. Place your shoulders directly over your wrists, your palms flat on the mat, and your feet hip-distance apart. (If you have pain in your low back, shoulders, or arms, lower your knees to the mat.) Look down and slightly forward, keeping your neck long. Inhale and lengthen your spine.

**Dandasana Chaturanga** (Four-Limbed Staff Pose)

Exhale and bend your elbows as you slowly lower your entire body, keeping your back as straight as a wood plank. Hug your elbows toward your sides and pause when your upper and lower arms form a right angle. Look down and slightly ahead. As you hold this challenging posture, you will feel yourself heating up. (If you were in Plank Pose, keep your knees on the mat and lower your upper body.)

**Urdhva Mukha Svanasana** (Upward-Facing Dog Pose)

In *Urdhva Mukha Svanasana*, inhale and draw your chest forward and up as you roll forward over your toes onto the tops of your feet. Keep your legs strong but your gluteal muscles relaxed by pressing the tops of your toes into the mat. Pull your shoulders back and expand your collarbones. Look straight ahead or slightly upward. (Instead of rolling over your toes, lift and place your feet on the mat one at a time. If this backbend is too challenging, switch to *Bhu-jhang-asana* or Cobra Pose.)

**Adho Mukha Svanasana** (Downward-Facing Dog)

In Downward-Facing Dog, exhale as you lift your hips up and back. Press your knuckles down, lengthen your back, and release your heels toward the mat. (Don't worry if your heels don't contact the mat. Allow your heels to feel heavy. Bend your knees as much as necessary if your hamstrings are tight.) Stay here for a few breaths.

**Anjaneyasana** (Low Lunge)

Step your left foot forward between your hands into *Anjaneyasana* at the end of your exhale and just before you inhale. Bring your right foot forward quickly, next to your left. If you are performing more than one round of *Surya Namaskar*, alternate which foot you step forward with each round.

**Arya Uttanasana** (Half Standing Forward Bend)

Take a deep breath and stand in *Ardha Uttanasana* with your chest raised halfway.

**Uttanasana** (Standing Forward Bend) (Standing Forward Bend)

In *Uttanasana*, bend forward at the hips while exhaling.

**Hastasana Urdhva** (Upward Salute)

Take a deep breath and enter *Urdhva Hastasana* again, reaching your arms overhead and out to the sides.

**Tadasana** (Mountain Pose) (Mountain Pose)

With your hands clasped at your heart or sides, exhale and perform *Tadasana* again. Continue your Sun Salutation or take a few breaths here while sensing and experiencing the bliss.

We strongly advise consulting an experienced and expert Vedic astrologer for professional assessment of your horoscope and further guidance. Please watch YouTube videos for correct pronuciation of the Chalisa, mantras, chants etc.

## AUSPICIOUS MANTRAS FOR THE TWELVE ZODIAC SIGNS

Write down the mantra that corresponds with your zodiac sign and keep it close to you so that you can refer to it as and when needed.

- Aries: ***OM HREEN SHREEN LAKSHMEE NAARAAYANAAY NAMAH***
- Taurus: ***OM GOPAALAAY UTTAR DHVAJAAY NAMAH***
- Gemini: ***OM KLEEN KRSHNAAY NAMAH***
- Cancer: ***OM HIRANY GARBHAAY AVYAKT ROOPINE NAMAH***
- Leo: ***OM KLEEN BRAHMAANE JAGADAADHAARAAY NAMAH***
- Virgo: ***OM NAMO PREEN PEETAAMBARAAY NAMAH***
- Libra: ***OM TATTV NINRANAAY TAARAKARAAMAAY NAMAH***
- Scorpio: ***OM NAARAAYANAAY SURASINHAAY NAMAH***
- Sagittarius: ***OM SHREEN DEVAKRSHNAAY ROODHRVASHOOTAAY NAMAH***

We strongly advise consulting an experienced and expert Vedic astrologer for professional assessment of your horoscope and further guidance. Please watch YouTube videos for correct pronuciation of the Chalisa, mantras, chants etc.

- Capricorn: ***OM SHREEN VATSALAAY NAMAH***
- Aquarius: ***OM SHREEN UPENDRAAY ACHYUTAAY NAMAH***
- Pisces: ***OM KLEEN UDDHRTAAY UDDHAARINE NAMAH***

We strongly advise consulting an experienced and expert Vedic astrologer for professional assessment of your horoscope and further guidance. Please watch YouTube videos for correct pronuciation of the Chalisa, mantras, chants etc.

# Other Books by the Author

This short religious book is a tribute to *Shani Dev* (the God of the planet Saturn) and is heavily influenced by *Vedic* astrology. Everyone will have the planet Saturn transit through their horoscope/birth-charts at least once or twice in their lifetime. These transitions could have various negative consequences about personal, professional, financial, and health issues. Signs of an unfavorable Saturn transitioning through your horoscope include, but are not limited to,

We strongly advise consulting an experienced and expert Vedic astrologer for professional assessment of your horoscope and further guidance. Please watch YouTube videos for correct pronuciation of the Chalisa, mantras, chants etc.

inexplicable anxiety, headaches, stress, morbidity, monetary crisis, loss of loved ones, accidents, unemployment, and so on.

This book is a collection of *Shani Chalisa, Shani Aarti, Shani Maha Mantra, Shani Beej Mantra, Shani Gayatri Mantra, Shani Mool Mantra, Dasaratha Krutha, Shani Stotram* and *Shani Vrat Katha* in both Hindi and English (along with their transliteration and meaning). Various practical and straightforward remedies (including Lal Kitab remedies) to mitigate the effects of Saturn's unfavorable transit through your horoscope have been listed in the book for easy reference. We hope that anyone who seeks *Shani Dev's* blessings will receive help from them.

We strongly advise consulting an experienced and expert Vedic astrologer for professional assessment of your horoscope and further guidance. Please watch YouTube videos for correct pronuciation of the Chalisa, mantras, chants etc.